SHE'S
NICE
THOUGH

Also by Mia Mercado

Weird But Normal

SHE'S NICE THOUGH

Essays on Being Bad at Being Good

MIA MERCADO

HarperOne
An Imprint of HarperCollins*Publishers*

The following essays were previously published in some form, and have been printed here with permission from the original publisher:

"What Does It Mean When a Girl Is Quiet?" on *The Rumpus*, published August 21, 2018; "Here to Make Friends" contains an excerpt from "Old Movies, Shows That Haven't Aged Well" on the *Washington Post*'s *The Lily*, published December 30, 2019; "Apologies for Men" on WICF Daily, published January 19, 2019; "Naughty List" on The Belladonna Comedy, published December 19, 2019.

The questions on pages 11–22 were taken from a *New York Times* Modern Love article that sourced from a study by Arthur Aron et al., "The Experimental Generation of Interpersonal Closeness," *Personality and Social Psychology Bulletin* 23, no. 4 (April 1997): 363–77, https://journals.sagepub.com/doi/pdf/10.1177/014 6167297234003.

HarperCollins books may be purchased for educational, business, or sales promotional use. For information, please email the Special Markets Department at SPsales@harpercollins.com.

FIRST EDITION

Designed by THE COSMIC LION

Library of Congress Cataloging-in-Publication Data has been applied for.

ISBN 978-0-06-309851-0

22 23 24 25 26 LSC 10 9 8 7 6 5 4 3 2 1

For anyone who is kinder than they have to be.
And whoever figured out how to make
sparkling water taste like that.

Contents

PART 1: Nice for What

Nice for What   3

Bad Answers to Good Questions and Vice Versa   11

How to Be Nice   23

A Strange and Unprecedented Time   26

Little Miss Shithead   36

Things That Are So Bad They're Good   42

Scary Stories to Keep You Up at Night   45

PART 2: Yellow Fever

Nice Girls Finish Eventually   51

What Does It Mean When a Girl Is Quiet?   57

How to Wife   60

Yellow Fever   67

Women for Decoration   73

PART 3: Here to Make Friends

It Girl   85

Can I Sit Here?   92

Here to Make Friends   100

CONTENTS

Kill Them with Kindness and Other
Imagined Crime Podcasts   109

Like and Subscribe   113

Don't Meet Your Enemies   124

PART 4: Good Girl, Bad Bitch

I'm the Bad Guy   133

Good Girl, Bad Bitch   140

Apologies for Men   151

Naughty List   153

Mandatory Fun   159

She's Friendly   162

Shy: F.A.Q.   172

PART 5: Mind Your Manners

Midwest Nice   177

If You Need Anything, My Name Is Mia   180

To Hell and Back   184

Mother May I?   192

Mind Your Manners   195

Ways I Will Die Because I Don't
Want to Be Rude and Ask for Help   208

Acknowledgments   213

PART 1

Nice for What

NICE FOR WHAT

I've never needed to be reminded to play nice. It is at the core of who I am and who I think I'm expected to be. I keep extra gum in my coat pockets. I've loaned out more hair ties than I'd ever be able to count. I've always assumed kindness, generosity, politeness, and goodness are one and the same, but now, I'm not so sure. I've been trying to figure out why I think my niceness is presumed—does it have to do with the fact that I'm Asian? A woman? The fact I'm an Asian woman and, in turn, so demure, so gentle, very "porcelain doll"? Is it because I'm from the Midwest and, were I to be mugged, I'd probably apologize for not having enough cash on hand? Does it have to do with how quiet I am, how small a space I feel I should take up, my instinct to fold inward and make myself the tiniest, innermost Russian nesting doll? What is it about my vibe that makes strangers trust me to watch their stuff while they go pee?? And, at the center of it all, am I *actually* nice or am I just performing a role I think I'm expected to play? Who is benefiting from my niceness?

It's hard not to be jaded by the fact that I often feel like my kindness is expected where others' is lauded. No one is shocked that I'm comfortable holding their baby. No one is surprised when I wait my turn, hold the door, remember to say *thank you* and *sorry* and *no, no, please,* you *should have the last piece.*

Most people describe my husband, Riley, as a nice person. He is tall, a man, white, handsome in a way that is approachable, funny in a way that makes you want to listen, and he has whatever Myers-Briggs type is most like a golden retriever. He makes friends easily, often, and in pretty much any environment. Once, a work acquaintance thought I didn't like them because I didn't laugh hard enough at a joke they made. I only know this because they confided this to Riley, a person they had known for one (1) hour.

I'm sure it sounds like I'm resentful of the way people celebrate my husband for, say, picking up a piece of trash on the sidewalk or standing next to a toddler particularly well. That's only because . . . I am. I'm mad that his Nice Points go further than mine. I also know that maybe genuinely nice people don't keep track of their good deeds with, say, Nice Points.

I used to worry the only discernible thing about me was my agreeability. In lieu of developing a personality, I established myself as someone who wouldn't challenge, question, or nudge even in the slightest. What are my thoughts on *Walden* or transcendentalism as a whole? Whatever yours are, Mrs. Teacher! Do I like Good Charlotte's music? Sure, she sounds nice! In hindsight, I think I've had entire friendships where I just nodded a lot and gave them someone to walk with around Kohl's department store.

I've spent so long with a label that reads NICE plastered across my forehead, occasionally pressing down at the corners to make sure it sticks, that I've rarely stopped to wonder who put the label there in the first place. Only recently have I started to pick at the edges or think about what I'd look like with a label that says BOLD or FUN or DOUBLE-JOINTED. Only now, after having been alive for three decades, am I asking questions like, "Is it unkind to disagree with someone? Can I be angry and nice at the same time?"

I'm not known for my anger. If anything, I default to annoyed.

When people cut me off in traffic, I get nervous before I get mad. Would a mouse give the finger to a rattrap on wheels?

I did get a taste of rage when I started taking Wellbutrin—sometimes known as the hot, horny antidepressant. Though it's unsettling to know that a couple hundred milligrams of something can ignite the part of my brain that decides, "ME WANT FIGHT," it was admittedly fun to feel angry.

Anger made me present. It was so much more visceral than the damp malaise of depression. I contemplated picking a fight with an editor over email. Throwing eggs sounded fun. I didn't do either of those things, but the rush! How cathartic to put your whole self into a feeling and, then, push that feeling out into the world through a screech, a stomp, a knife through unspoken tension. Anyway, I'm no longer taking Wellbutrin on its own.

Recently, however, I felt something akin to my Wellbutrin rage when the collective public started going on their Asian Apology Tour. Amid the growing number of hate crimes against Asians and Asian Americans, in correlation with the pandemic, I got a handful of messages from friends, acquaintances, and virtual strangers alike to "check in." This trend, I'm assuming, was born out of non-Asian (often white, usually liberal) people wanting to do something actionable in response to these attacks. They wanted to speak out against the way Asian people, Chinese people in particular, were being vilified in conversations led by some (often white, usually conservative) people. They were looking for ways to step forward and be a barrier, shielding Asians from *those* white people. This also became a way—whether intentional or not—to step forward and distinguish themselves as "doing the work," as one of the good ones.

Online, I saw Asian people offering these kinds of check-ins as a way for non-Asian people to engage in an immediate, intimate capacity. And who wouldn't want to be offered solace? To feel seen in some small part? To have people acknowledge pain you've often felt you should keep private? I also saw Asian people who balked at the idea of a bunch of white strangers DMing them to say, "Thinking of you <3 Stop Asian hate!!"

I—and, I'm assuming, many others—fell somewhere in the middle. I wanted there to be recognition for the collective mourning that happens when you see people who look like you killed because of the way they look. I wanted people to feel bad for every joke they made about an Asian massage parlor and every time they laughed when they heard the words *me so horny*. I also wanted to be left alone by people I knew hadn't experienced this strange and specific kind of grief.

Fortunately—luckily?—I didn't have to confront any pointed violence in person. Though I had moments where I worried strangers would approach me in anger or avoid me out of fear—seeing my eyes above my mask and thinking, *Hmm, looks Asian enough to me!*—it was never something I experienced personally. No one yelled at me or steered clear of me. No one really brought up my race in connection to COVID at all aside from these apology messages I got.

Some messages were welcomed and within the context of an actual mutual relationship. They were from people I'd previously had conversations with about race and whiteness among many, many other conversations about life, work, my family, my dog, depression, wide-legged overalls, and the best kinds of soup. They were from people I'd be mad at—or, more likely, annoyed with—if they didn't text me on my birthday, people who know with certainty that I am talking about them right now. Other messages were . . . a surprise? Well-meaning and earnest, sure. But definitely a surprise.

Were these gestures *nice*? Were these people *nice*? Was the random stranger who slipped into my DMs to say, "Thinking of you," *nice*? If so, nice for what? Nice to what end? Nice for who? Why did niceness feel so much like a bribe? It made me wonder if niceness isn't a personality trait but a trading card.

In case you need it, here is a list of things I would *actually* like you to apologize to me, specifically, for:

1. A particular interaction between the two of us (e.g., you cut me off in a meeting, you ignored my email, you said a mean thing to me, you farted on me and walked away)
2. That's it. That's the whole list.

There is something so sad and so funny about getting messages that basically boiled down to "sorry about the racism :/ ." Though I'd never be bold enough to ask directly, I'm curious why they thought they were apologizing, who they thought that apology was for? As someone who says "sorry" like a reflex, I can sense when someone is expressing pointed remorse and when they're offering an apology as an obligatory act.

Some of those messages I responded to with a quick "thanks!"— (you can tell I was irritated because I only used the one exclamation point). Others, I ignored, panicking a little that they might be able to tell I read their message and didn't respond. (This is a near impossibility as I've never once had read receipt enabled on my phone. I still don't understand who that feature is for. The number of times I read a message, think about responding, and forget about it entirely only to wake up in the middle of the night four days later like *oh no* is none of your business!) I still don't know if I should have responded to those unexpected check-ins, setting aside my own comfort to preserve theirs. Half of me—probably the white half (JUST KIDDING!!!)—knows they were trying to be nice, to be good, to acknowledge the Bad Things happening rather than just ignore them. The other half called my sister immediately to be like, "Are you also hearing 'sorry' from random white people?"

Is it rude to ignore an unprompted apology? Should I have acted kindly and responded with gratitude? Would an equally obligatory "Thank you so much!" really have been a nice thing to say?

Those apology messages felt indicative of a much larger social tendency—both in cultural conversations and in myself—to *perform* kindness rather than actually figure out what it means to be "good." It's so much easier to do the right thing when you're being told what is right. Say "please" and "thank you" because your parents said you should. You can point to a commandment and say, "I haven't coveted my neighbor's wife, so I must be doing something right." Rules and guidelines and pretty Instagram infographics are easy. It's much harder to examine our innermost intentions and ask, "Who am I doing this for?"

I started thinking more about the cultural ramifications of niceness after I saw *Parasite*. There are plenty of reason to love that movie: there's the bop that is "Jessica, Only Child, Illinois, Chicago." There's the scene where the wealthy Park parents get freaky on the couch while the Kim family hides underneath the coffee table, equal parts horny and terrifying. There's the fact that Da-song, the Parks' youngest child, is just chilling with an arrow between his butt cheeks when "Jessica"/Ki-jung first meets him. But it's how Chung-sook, the matriarch of the Kim family, responds to her husband describing the Parks as nice "even though [they're] rich" that I cannot get out of my head. As the Kims secretly party in the Parks' lush living room, drinking their fancy booze and eating their snacks, Chung-sook half-drunkenly replies, "She's nice *because* she's rich."

I'd never really thought about how social niceties are a privilege to be able to both experience and give out. There's a certain brand of niceness that seems inextricable from servitude, particularly when any kind of imbalance of power is involved. If you are expected to be nice to someone who is more powerful than you, it's likely obedience rather than human kindness.

And so, I guess, I'm mostly curious, when I'm nice, who am I being nice to? What am I being nice for?

Why be nice to the man at the pool who insists he knows I'm Asian, who doesn't wait for an answer, anyway, because he says he can tell by my "kung fu stare"? Why placate the men at the bar who won't leave me alone until I tell them my race? Why oblige the guy on the metro who asks for my number because he "could tell" I was half-Filipina? Why feel an added level of obligation to engage because all these men are Asian?

So much of kindness comes down to the ability to absorb the thoughtlessness of others. I wonder if people would still think I'm nice if I spoke up when I felt uncomfortable. On the other side, I wonder who has soaked up my own verbal slights like a sponge, filling their pores with my thoughtless detritus so I can keep believing that I am good.

I mean, it's certainly helped my own ego in the past couple years to be a nice and good rule follower. I kept my six-foot distance without complaint. I wore my mask over my nose. I felt better about myself when I wore my mask through the drive-through, a momentary signal to the person working: *Don't worry. I'm one of the good ones.* I did wonder what being quarantined had done to our tolerance for doling out these kinds of niceties, but I suppose we have our answer. How will people recant stories of the time they started a fight on an airplane because they didn't want to follow CDC health regulations? How will the rest of us talk about the time we cheered at a viral video of a flight attendant duct-taping a belligerent, unmasked passenger to a seat? Maybe the only feeling more visceral than anger is righteousness.

I wonder why it's taken me this long to question the motivation of my own kindness, but it has felt more critical than ever to differentiate between the performance of niceness and that which comes from true good intentions.

I don't think I'm any less agreeable than I was a year ago, two years ago, thirty years ago. I don't think I'm any less primed to shrink or apologize or smile out of obligation than I've been before. But when I push back against things that make me uncomfortable—the things that seem rooted in surface-level obligation, the things that reinforce ideas I wish didn't exist in the first place—I'm starting not to worry about it as much. And worrying less feels nice.

BAD ANSWERS TO GOOD QUESTIONS AND VICE VERSA

The following are a list of questions published in the New York Times. *They are purported to make even a perfect stranger fall in love with you, and so I am answering them for you, dear reader, because those 5-star reviews aren't going to write themselves.*

Given the choice of anyone in the world, whom would you want as a dinner guest?

The person who wrote these questions. I'd ask that person if it also works if you answer the questions *at* the other person (e.g., someone reading a book). Like a magic spell or a witch's curse. Then, we'd order mozzarella sticks.

Would you like to be famous? In what way?

No. I don't want to be famous, as evidenced by the fact that I wrote down, in a book, "I do not want to be famous." Nothing makes someone less famous than writing a book. In what way? Um, I guess, platonically?

Before making a telephone call, do you ever rehearse what you are going to say? Why?

Do people . . . *not* do this? I had to re-record my outgoing voice-mail message at least six times. And still, I had a friend leave me a voice mail—don't worry, I pressed charges—where they said, "Were you crying when you recorded your voice-mail message? Why do you sound so sad?? I forgot what I was even calling to ask you about." I rehearse what I'm going to say before a phone call because, if I don't, I fear I'll forget how to put words in an order that makes sense to other people and end up saying something like, "Can I get a tooth date with the mouth doctor, por favor?"

What would constitute a "perfect" day for you?

My perfect day is food-centric. For breakfast, I have an oat milk latte with some bullshit flavoring like vanilla lavender or hazelnut symphony. I don't feel embarrassed saying "oat milk" out loud. I have an everything bagel with veggie cream cheese. The bagel can be from anywhere because I haven't developed a palate for fancy bagels in the middle of the country. I have had bouts of depression cured by objectively bad bagels.

For lunch, I probably have some kind of salad and sandwich. That sounds kinda cute of me to do, right? The salad consists of seven, perfectly portioned bites, which is the most bites it should take to eat any salad. Each bite has a crouton, goat cheese, spicy pecan, maybe a craisin, and a little leaf and is drenched in some kind of dressing that makes Riley go, "What stinks?" I love a chicken salad sandwich or a veggie sandwich with some kind of spicy garlic aioli. I am a mayo queen, and I will be taking no further questions on that. After lunch, time stops as I take a three-hour nap.

For dinner, I make obscene love to a pasta dish. The best pasta shapes are cavatappi and rigatoni. The pasta comes with Olive Garden breadsticks, which are delicious, disgusting, and functional. With dinner, I have my new favorite cocktail, which is Limoncello and vodka topped with LimonCello LaCroix. It tastes like a hot Italian waiter flirting with a lemon meringue pie.

As a digestif, I take an edible and eat a bag of microwave popcorn while watching the absolute worst movie I can find. At this point, I realize I didn't have any kind of sweet treat all day! A crime! I gorge myself on KitKats and Reese's Peanut Butter Cups before realizing I have a slice of tres leches cake in the fridge. I eat that in bed with my Bed Sparkly, a sparkling water that I drink in bed. (Throughout the day, I have had anywhere between two and seven sparkling waters. Healthy!) I play Spider Solitaire on my phone until I pass out.

When did you last sing to yourself? To someone else?

Right nooOOOow. (Buy the audiobook to hear me sing!)

If you were able to live to the age of ninety and retain either the mind or body of a thirty-year-old for the last sixty years of your life, which would you want?

Mind because I don't know where I'd keep a body for that long.

Do you have a secret hunch about how you will die?

What I love about this question is it was absolutely not written by someone who has ever been depressed or knows the feeling of waking up like, "Oh, great. This bitch again." There have been many days I've had a secret hunch about how I'll die because the murder call is coming from inside the depression house. Ultimately, I will either die from *Thelma and Louise*-ing myself off a cliff or starvation after seeing how long our dog, Ava, would obsessively lick the back of my hand if I never told her to stop.

Name three things you and your partner appear to have in common.

For the purposes of this class project, you and I are partners. Three things we have in common: we can both read, we're both Virgos— I'm a Virgo, which is a dominant trait and becomes the zodiac sign for all other parties present—and we are both wondering whether it's legal for me to basically answer a fancy Myspace quiz and call it a chapter of my book.

For what in your life do you feel most grateful?

My family, my friends, Riley (he's family but also my intern), Ava (she's family but also my boss); being in my thirties—now the hottest age to be; therapy, SSRIs and antidepressants; nice weather; having the time to take a nap; my favorite spoon (it's flat on the tip, which makes it perfect for getting every last bit of ice cream); living in a time when there are so many bad movies and TV shows I can watch on demand instead of ever having to pretend I want to watch *Citizen Kane*; comfy clothes; having the freedom to worry about stupid things because that means the big things are taken care of; Blue Bell's Bride's Cake ice cream.

If you could change anything about the way you were raised, what would it be?

I would want to have been a twin.

Take four minutes and tell your partner your life story in as much detail as possible.

Okay, if you want to tell me your life story, I'll listen. Time starts now.

If you could wake up tomorrow having gained any one quality or ability, what would it be?

Wait, did you finish telling me your life story? You're reading a whole-ass book about me and my thoughts and don't want to spend four minutes talking about yourself? Are you, like, obsessed with me? Tell me who you had a crush on in eighth grade, coward. Oh, and if I could wake up with any new ability, I'd want to be instantly double-jointed. (1) It's kind of gross and (2) then, I would never have to panic to think of a fun fact during icebreaker introductions ever again.

If a crystal ball could tell you the truth about yourself, your life, the future, or anything else, what would you want to know?

I'd wish for more wishes.

Is there something that you've dreamed of doing for a long time? Why haven't you done it?

I have this recurring dream where I'm in a mall and sorting through lots of huge, empty Tupperware containers. I think I heard once that it's common for people to dream about being in a nondescript mall and meandering through rooms that are kind of like stores but not really. Why haven't I done it? Because going to a mall as an adult is something I have to mentally, emotionally, and physically prepare for. It's like being in a giant McDonald's PlayPlace, but instead of getting trapped in the ball pit, you get stuck in the combined smell vortex from Abercrombie & Fitch, Aéropostale, and Hollister.

What is the greatest accomplishment of your life?

Only having pooped my pants once as an adult and writing two books.

What do you value most in a friendship?

Someone who has the same sense of humor as me and better snacks at their house.

What is your most treasured memory?

Hmm, no thanks. Let's list some of my favorite foods from movies and TV shows instead: the green sorbet palate cleanser in *Princess Diaries*; the imaginary food in *Hook* that looks like rainbow-colored mashed potatoes; Mary-Kate and Ashley Olsen in *Billboard Dad* scrambling eggs in a giant clear plastic bag because it's easier than whisking them; the ruffled chips and onion dip Mila Kunis eats in *Honey, We Shrunk Ourselves*; the pancakes in *Teletubbies*; the cheese pizza in *A Goofy Movie*; the candy wrapper American Lindsay Lohan crinkles to pretend her phone call is breaking up in *The Parent Trap*; the Oreos dunked in peanut butter in *The Parent Trap*.

What is your most terrible memory?

While I was thinking about movie food, I remembered the sensation of squooshing Go-Gurt out of its tube and cutting the sides of my mouth on the hard plastic edge. That was pretty terrible.

If you knew that in one year you would die suddenly, would you change anything about the way you are now living? Why?

Honestly? Probably not. Maybe I'd audition for a reality show because I'd have a really good built-in sob story. Other than that, I probably just wouldn't let anyone talk to me about superhero franchises ever again. My time is too precious.

What does friendship mean to you?

Does everyone have the thing where they don't feel close to someone until they talk shit with you? My friendship love language is talking shit. Not in a malicious way. Something just feels biologically reassuring whenever someone feels comfortable griping about an inconsequential, shared complaint. Misery loves company and, like, I *love*

Misery. It's so fun, so nice. But sometimes it can be . . . a little much, you know?

What roles do love and affection play in your life?

Um, is this quiz flirting with me?

Alternate sharing something you consider a positive characteristic of your partner. Share a total of five items.

Okay, you do me first. Wow! That's so nice! Really? Oh my god, stop! Aww, thank you! Five positive characteristics about you: (1) You give really good compliments (2) You're a great listener (3) You pay attention to me (4) You bought or borrowed this book and (5) If you stole this book, that sucks but I guess I'm a little flattered?

How close and warm is your family? Do you feel your childhood was happier than most other people's?

A while back, my dad digitized all our old home videos. We have dozens and dozens of hours of footage of our family, especially when my siblings and I were little, because my dad would send videos to his parents in the Philippines as a way to stay in touch. That feels a little less special now, when there are babies who do sponsored posts on TikTok and people who make Instagram accounts for their fetuses. But I've learned it's more rare among people my age, when you only had so many photos you could take on a roll of film or so many minutes you could record on a camcorder's tape.

After my dad put our home videos on DVDs, our family would occasionally watch home movies when we wanted to have something on TV but didn't have anything in particular we wanted to watch. It was part nostalgia, part narcissism, part comfort. It's so strange to see smaller versions of yourself saying things you can't imagine yourself ever saying, acting in ways that feel both nothing like you've ever been and exactly how you'll always be. There's a video of me painting a shoebox in the backyard with my brothers and sister. I'm probably six or seven. I ask my mom, who's recording, if she likes what I'm making. She says "yes" and I tell her, "I think it's gonna be reeeeally neeeeeat." I say my Es with a nasal quality I'll never be able to perfectly replicate. The clip so quickly encapsulates so much of who I am: a little oversincere, sometimes performatively so; kind of annoying; extremely midwestern; bad at visual art. It's also strange to see videos of my parents from when they were my age. It's like seeing a celebrity take out the trash. Parents, they're just like us!

For a while, my family couldn't stop quoting ourselves from the home videos. Sometimes they were in context, mostly not. At my wedding, one of our photographers was gathering my immediate family for a picture, and my dad, quoting a thing Ana said when she was small, jokingly said, "Don't shoot, Mom and Dad, okay?!" And I was like, "Dad, that is not a thing you can just say out of context." Those are the times I feel closest to my family, when we're using familial shorthand and forget the rest of the world around us. When we're saying things that only we would get.

How do you feel about your relationship with your mother?

How do *you* feel about *your* relationship with *your* mother? See how that sounds? Let's lead with kindness, okay?

Make three true "we" statements each. For instance, "We are both in this room feeling . . ."

We are both looking at these words right now. We are both wondering whether I'm going to say something that alienates at least one person reading this book. We both have good taste in books.

BAD ANSWERS TO GOOD QUESTIONS AND VICE VERSA

Complete this sentence: "I wish I had someone with whom I could share . . ."

Identical DNA. I want a twin so bad! How could I not? The 1990s and early 2000s were Twin City (not to be confused with the Twin Cities). We had Mary-Kate and Ashley Olsen, American and British Lindsay Lohan, Tia and Tamera Mowry. Finding out Aaron Carter has a twin sister makes me like him more. Knowing that Rami Malek has a twin is not the kind of information I should be trusted with. Learning that someone has a twin makes me think of them differently, like finding out someone goes by their middle name or isn't really a "sweets person."

If you were going to become a close friend with your partner, please share what would be important for him or her to know.

It's too late for me to try to care about *Star Wars*. I'll go see the new ones if that's important to you, but my brain just does not have the capacity to have strong feelings about the franchise. I didn't watch any of the movies growing up so there isn't that nostalgic element for me, something I think is required to feel beholden to *Star Wars*. My only feelings are Oscar Isaac is hot, John Boyega is hot, Carrie Fisher is hot and a godsend, and Baby Yoda is cute but looks like he stinks.

Tell your partner what you like about them; be very honest this time, saying things that you might not say to someone you've just met.

I feel like we've already done this at least twice in these questions. How about instead we try to figure out what part of my brain is broken in a way that, recently, when I saw a WE'RE HIRING sign at Taco

Bell, I had a split second where I thought, *Should I . . . quit everything and manage a Taco Bell?*

Share with your partner an embarrassing moment in your life.

No, I'm too shy! Just kidding. I've written many of them down in this book. Take your pick.

Just for you, partner, here is a deep-cut embarrassing moment: On that high school church trip, I was lying about falling in snow and I actually peed my pants laughing.

When did you last cry in front of another person? By yourself?

Today. Whenever you're reading this, the answer for both questions is today. I like crying! It feels good! I know I'm not a healthy person because if I were ever required to cry on camera, I know exactly what sad things I would conjure to make myself tear up: the idea of Ava someday dying; that one part of the song "Gravity" by Sara Bareilles—if you've heard the song, you know which part; or the scene in *A Cinderella Story* where the stepsisters read Hilary Duff's journal during a school play.

Tell your partner something that you like about them already.

Really, again?! Okay, I like that you are reading this book. I mean that sincerely. I don't take for granted the fact that I have space to talk about what I like and hate, what I feel and think, what I wish people talked more about, what I wish people did less, what kind of pasta shapes are the best.

What, if anything, is too serious to be joked about?

I've never understood the very trite idea that poking fun at everything is actually the highest form of inclusivity. It's got big "I'm not a bigot—I hate everyone!" graphic tee energy. If you're making a joke, specifically about a group of people of which you are not a member, where the setup and punch line rely on stereotypes, that isn't really a joke. It's just repeating that stereotype with the words rearranged. Also, no one can joke about bacon anymore. Not because it's too serious but because a while back, it became this weird comedy shortcut where saying people like bacon passed as a joke. The 2010s were wild.

If you were to die this evening with no opportunity to communicate with anyone, what would you most regret not having told someone? Why haven't you told them yet?

I would regret not telling Jeff Bezos he sucks shit. I haven't told him because I'm not yet ready to be suspended from Twitter.

Your house, containing everything you own, catches fire. After saving your loved ones and pets, you have time to safely make a final dash to save any one item. What would it be? Why?

Because I don't have any precious heirlooms or other irreplaceable sentimental items that come to mind, I'd probably grab my phone purely for logistical purposes. How else would I call 911? How would I file an insurance claim? How would I google "How do you file an insurance claim"?

Of all the people in your family, whose death would you find most disturbing? Why?

I feel like this answer could be used in a court of law should anyone in my family die and they are not the person I list. So . . . you didn't think it'd be disturbing if your third cousin died? And now they've been extremely murdered. Hmm, seems suspicious.

Share a personal problem and ask your partner's advice on how he or she might handle it. Also, ask your partner to reflect back to you how you seem to be feeling about the problem you have chosen.

So, what I'm learning from these questions is that the way to make someone fall in love with you is by having a minitherapy session. I mean, I don't disagree. A big part of Riley and my relationship is me asking him "Am I bad?" and him saying "No," which is a lot quicker and much cheaper than the fifty-five-minute sessions where I'm asking my therapist the same thing just in a more long-winded way. Anyway, have you found a dandruff shampoo you like?

HOW TO BE NICE

None of us are born nice. I know it's hard to hear, but it's true. We emerge into the world selfish little goblins desperate to get our grubby paws on anything and everything. Fortunately, we can learn the ways of human kindness with a few of these helpful tips and just four easy payments of $39.99. Ha ha, just kidding! That's tip number one: make a little joke to ease any tension. If that doesn't work, try giving them four easy payments of $39.99.

Nothing says "nice" like you, walking around, saying, "I'M NICE." Give this a try whenever you want to make sure the people around you know they can depend on you should they need a little kindness. Like, a shoulder to cry on or someone to hold the door open for them even though they're kind of far away and will feel obligated to do that little half run.

Nice people do nice things without being asked. For example, you could throw away trash you see on the street. You could wipe off the water-splattered sink in a public restroom. You could try giving a wedgie to everyone who asks you questions like, "So, where are you *really* from?" or "But if *I* can't say that word, how come *they* can say it?" You'd be doing them a favor because people who say things like that are asking for a wedgie.

Make sure to acknowledge other people—a classic sign of niceness.

A friendly wave on the street is an excellent start. But often a simple "hey" or "hello" or "I like your shirt . . . I said, I LIKE YOUR SHIRT. NO, YOUR *SHIRT*. Okay, you too" will do.

Nice people love to smile. Let's see your smile! Oh, okay. Maybe a little less teeth. Wait, a little more. Maybe try a closemouthed smi— That's somehow worse. Have you heard of smizing? That's where you make someone else smile by giving them french fries. Is there anything nicer than unexpected free fries?

Another way to be nice is to slip the number "69" into conversation. Whenever I do that, people always say, "Nice."

Be helpful! Nice people are helpful, and helpful people are nice. If you see someone drop their bag, help them pick it up. If you notice someone's got something in their teeth, consider telling them. Ultimately, you won't tell them because you don't want them to worry about how long they've had that thing stuck in their teeth. Was it there during the big meeting? When they were flirting with the barista? You're doing them a bigger, kinder favor by ignoring it altogether and letting them panic about it later when they're alone.

Nice people ask how others are feeling. Try checking in with those around you every so often. Are they happy? Sad? Fine? "Fine"? That's where someone asks how you are, but you don't want to go into it. You could also check if they're updog. That's where you're pretending to understand a joke you don't get but are too embarrassed to have it explained.

Nice people have safe words to make sure everyone is comfortable and having a good time. It could be an obscure forest creature, the name of your favorite Jonas Brother, or really any word you want. Mine is *updog*.

Now, if you're thinking about just moving to Nice, France, as a loophole . . . congrats! You found it! The secret shortcut to being Nice!

What someone considers "nice" can be a bit subjective. So feel free to experiment with it a bit, play around in the space. When they say, "jump," you say, "yes and!" If they ask for a hand, give them a round of applause and then say, "Oh, I'm just pulling your leg . . . I mean, your HAND!" and yank their fingers really hard.

One thing that will always be a nice gesture is baking someone a pie. Who doesn't love a pie? Of course, now comes the obvious questions: What kind of pie? Any kind, really! Apple, blueberry, cherry, strawberry rhubarb, humble pie, one baked with four and twenty blackbirds, one with plums but don't let that little shit Jack Horner get his thumbs into it, even key lime.

If you're stuck, try looking to other nice people. You can tell someone is nice if they smile a lot, listen intently, are the main character's best friend, earnestly say things like, "Oh, hon!," or are Tom Hanks.

Finally, nice people are nice because they *want* to be, not because they have to be or as some perverse dare their football friends put them up to. An easy place to start is by thinking about how you'd want others to treat you. Would you want them to be kind? Considerate? An asshole? A bitch? A lover? A child? A mother? A joker? A smoker? A midnight toker?

If that doesn't work, you can always just say "69."

A STRANGE AND UNPRECEDENTED TIME

THE BEFORE ERA

At the beginning of 2020, I was prepared for a busy year. One filled with book events, readings, parties, travel, and general whimsy. I was months away from being a published author! I was thinking about pitching a second book (the one you are currently reading—it remains a product of one of the few highlights from that year: being told that yeah, sure, I can write another book). I was ready for fortune and fame or at least the opportunity to posit, "Is everyone I've ever had a crush on going to read my book and finally love me back?"

I was turning thirty, something that felt important or at least felt like it *should* feel important. I think I feel the same amount of panic everyone feels about getting older; it's inevitable and there is some comfort in having a shared experience with pretty much every other person who has come before me. Also, I'd heard that, in your thirties, you suddenly stop giving so much of a shit. Maybe the Time Fairy would grant me the gall to care just a little bit less.

I was starting to feel Grown. Like I had evolved to a more finished form. Not the final boss, but the boss before the final boss. The one who is scrappier and seems like they have less to lose. I bought a blazer. I hired a tax person. Riley and I signed up for a Southwest credit card because of all the miles we would earn from all the travel we were about to do. LOL, and furthermore, ha ha.

I will start by saying that our pandemic experience was much easier and more low-key than most. The two of us, our friends, and family all stayed pretty healthy. Staying inside wasn't so much a punishment as it was permission to do a thing I already wanted to do. I had enough writing jobs at the time that we didn't feel a huge financial hit when I released a book during a very bad year for book releases. Riley, who teaches eighth-grade math, had his school year canceled and was being paid not to do his job—great for the two of us in the immediate future, horrible for one million other, much more consequential reasons. We have a house and a yard. We have a dog and like being around each other. We had very few obstacles when it came to staying safe and relatively sane.

And it was all still *really fucking exhausting*.

Under the assumption that you are as nosy as I am and would have loved a live feed of everyone inside their homes during the pandemic—if you're also wondering, How did people cope? What did they binge-watch? What did they stock up on? Was everyone else also awash with a general malaise? Did they know what Zoom was before March 2020?—I present to you a retrospective account of that very strange and unprecedented time.

THE PRECIPICE

In early March, an hour before I was set to go to the airport for a trip to Los Angeles, the person I was going to see called and said, "Oh, good, you haven't left yet. Don't." It was among the most unsettling phone calls I've ever received. Though it was starting to seep into the coastal cities, few if any coronavirus cases had hit Kansas City or the Midwest.

"Should we, like, buy beans or something?" I asked Riley. We did, but I'm pretty sure it was the same amount of beans we would usually buy. That first trip to the grocery store felt overly precautious—I mean, nothing was *really* happening in our immediate vicinity just yet. We grabbed a few other essentials—toilet paper, LaCroix, some stupid flavor of chip I saw like, "Spicy Ranch, U Dumb Lil Skank"— and headed home, feeling a little silly but at least we had chips.

Then came the predictions. The warnings. The questions about whether we should be wearing masks. The last time Riley and I ate inside a restaurant in 2020, I remember saying, "I think we should be conscientious about how much we touch the menu and table." Something that would have had me committed had I said it just a few days before.

OH, OKAY, IT'S HAPPENING

You know something is going on when nearly every email you receive—from family, coworkers, brand newsletters, promo blasts, PR messages from sex toy companies—starts in a nearly identical way: *Hope you're doing well considering [gestures wildly] all this.* The world was coming to an end, yet I knew if I opened my in-box, I'd still see an email from Bath and Body Works offering three-for-one hand soap—with antibacterial microbes!

It was mid-March, and the whiteboards outside of Costco said they were out of toilet paper, hand sanitizer, disinfecting wipes, flour, the will to live, etc. Riley and I made sure we had multiple masks in our car in case we went somewhere, like the grocery store or . . . a different grocery store. We started getting acquainted with what six feet apart looks like. We stopped shaking hands, hugging, standing too close, feeling the need to make small talk with acquaintances who were also trying to figure out if a thirty-six-pack of toilet paper was enough to last them a week.

The beans were gone. The pasta was ravished. I write this specifically to remember how apocalyptic it felt. How surreal it was to be standing outside a supermarket, masked and sanitized, waiting to be let in by an employee monitoring shopper head count.

On St. Patrick's Day, my sister, Ana, called me from Northern California, where she was temporarily working on a farm. She asked if I thought she should leave, lest she be stuck there for the rest of the year. I know this makes me sound like a great-aunt saying, "Back in my day, we could get a nice steak dinner for a nickel," but we booked a flight from San Francisco to Kansas City for the next day, and it only cost $99. I hate to say it but that exceedingly cheap flight was the first time I really stopped and thought—*wait, what?* I had a moment of realization, like, "Oh, something is really happening."

After she arrived in March, Ana stayed with us for a large part of quarantine. It's the longest we've gotten to live together since I lived at home, which was nice and hard and helped make the months feel less horrifying. Our self-isolated household consisted of me, Riley, Ana, Ava (our dog), the garden Ana started, the compost bin she also started, and Ana's kombucha SCOBY who she named Christy Carlson Romano. I love my crunchy-granola sister and her menagerie of nonhuman life.

BREAD

We did not participate in the sourdough craze of spring 2020, but I'd argue that Ana made more beer bread during that time than everyone else combined. She perfected the art of bread risen via shitty, gross beer. She got experimental with it, once using a mango beer to see how it would turn out. (Bad.) Another time, the bread was so salty it seemed like she was pulling a prank, even on herself—we still don't fully understand how the salty loaf came to be.

While Ana was creating things with her hands and an oven, and while everyone else was falling in love with baking from scratch and tending to their sourdough starters, I rekindled my love for microwave popcorn. I forgot how good microwave popcorn can be. Is movie theater popcorn simultaneously the best and most disgusting kind of popcorn? No, but it's good and doesn't require you to heat up oil or pump some viscous neon yellow liquid labeled "butter," quotes included.

Did you know that the first food intentionally cooked by a microwave was popcorn? I did not until 2020, when I was stuck at home, chomping through bags upon bags of the stuff, and got bored enough to google "popcorn button on microwave why?" To be honest, I, too, would figure out how to invent something to make it easier to turn hard corn kernels into the fluffy, salty, buttery delicacy that is popcorn.

Microwave popcorn could cure my depression. It turns a terrible movie into . . . still a terrible movie—but with popcorn! In college, my comfort food of choice was microwave popcorn and Ritz crackers, a texture combination I still find incredible. During quarantine, I sought any and all forms of comfort. I snuck a few cans of black olives among our stack of beans. I watched *Gossip Girl*, which I hadn't actually seen until that point, but it still felt nostalgic. Any clothing item that didn't have "sweat" in the name would not grace my body. If the world was ending, I was going to be comfortable.

OKAY, I GUESS IT'S PUZZLES NOW

The three of us dabbled in jigsaw puzzles, and I quickly learned that my stamina for doing puzzles is exactly thirty minutes. I can stare at a disassembled puzzle for exactly half an hour before wanting to pull my eyes out of my head. I love doing puzzles in theory. I want to be there at the very beginning while we're dumping all the pieces out, touching the gross cardboard back and flipping over every single piece. I want to check in halfway through, like a dad who walks up to the grill and says to a different dad, "It's looking good." Then, I want to come back when a few dozen pieces are left and be there to watch the last piece get put in its place. Don't worry, I would never insist I put the last piece in as I wasn't present for the whole thing. I'm a selfish puzzler but not *that* selfish.

Though my puzzle stamina is limited, I do have strong opinions on the "right" way to do a puzzle. (I'm fun!) The correct way to start is, of course, by separating the edge pieces from the rest of the pieces. I assumed this was how everyone started their jigsaw puzzle journey, but it very clearly is not. Sometimes, while I was doing this, Riley would start assembling edge pieces he found that connected, and I'd get mad at him for "cheating." (Did I mention I'm fun?)

While jigsaw puzzles are a bit of a chore, I have no limit to my appetite for word puzzles. Word searches. Boggle. Scrambled vocabulary tests. I've destroyed relationships over a game of Scrabble. Thus, it was only a matter of time before I threw myself into the world of crossword puzzles. Fortunately, Riley already had the same affliction.

When I say we became obsessed with crossword puzzles, I need you to understand I mean this in a medical way. Not only have we done every single daily crossword on the *New York Times* website from January 2020 until present day, we've also done every archived Monday crossword (the easiest day to complete) dating back to 2010. We perfected the art of the Puns and Anagrams puzzle, a crossword puzzle where each answer is either, as the name suggests, a pun or an anagram based on the clue. We learned how to solve a Cryptic Crossword puzzle, which, I gotta be honest, sometimes seemed more like self-harm than enjoyment. When I got desperate and solving a Saturday was too hard, I'd do whatever daily crosswords I could get my virtual hands on. *USA Today. The New Yorker.* Vox. Sporcle. Dictionary.com. Crossword puzzles clearly created as school projects. A-plus, Jessica P.

Our crossword obsession quickly extended to an obsession with the *New York Times* Spelling Bee. It's a different word game that's kind of like Boggle without the time constraint. It's the perfect puzzle game if you like words, anagrams, and seeing if the *Times* accepts "doodoo" as a word. (They do not.)

GET A HOBBY, OKAY?

It became clear over the course of the pandemic that I do not know how to have a casual hobby. Either I do something once and hate it or I try it, love it, do it for hours on end, make it my personality, start a new life, devote it to the new hobby, marry the new hobby, have kids with the new hobby, and eventually die holding hands with the new hobby.

I was convinced I would hate cross-stitching, but boredom and a free cross-stitch kit made me try anyway. After the first few stitches, I fell in love. It was magical in a very practical way. It fed both parts of my brain: the chaotic half I have to control lest I draw with lipstick all over my face in the rare moments I feel bold enough to wear lipstick; and the other half that thrives on organization, on rules, on being allowed to think deep *inside* the box. Cross-stitching is basically paint-by-number but with thread! Why had no one told me this before?! You get to feel creative by picking which millions of colors of thread you want to use and finding a design that looks cool but isn't so difficult you'll try to stab yourself with your needle. But you have to weave the thread in a specific way to create the cute little "x." I love a craft with parameters!

People capable of looking at construction paper, markers, glitter, and glue sticks and coming up with something to make are functioning on a completely different plane than I am. I'd probably end up just using the marker and paper to write an apology letter to whoever organized this crafting event. "My deepest condolences, but I need structure and guidance. Otherwise, I will most certainly end up making something that looks phallic, which may or may not be intentional. Unfortunately, when given the space to explore my creativity, my brain goes 'peepee, poopoo, draw a butt.' I do not wish to subject you to that. Thus, I will bid you adieu."

Like every other hobby I've picked up in an obsessive way, I woke up one morning and realized, *I don't love you anymore.*

Cross-stitching and I are no longer together in a romantic sense, but there are no bad feelings between us. We catch up every once in a while when I open the desk drawer in our spare room and see the two different half-finished projects I've sadly cast aside, both with a needle still embedded like I may pick it back up at any moment. Maybe one day we can reunite but, for now, I think I need my space.

Also, I found out I actually love *Mario Kart*, despite previously thinking I hated it on account of . . . being very bad at it. I think Waluigi and I have something really special.

OKAY, YEP, STILL HAPPENING

I couldn't tell you exactly what I did between June 2020 and March 2021. Nothing? Everything? I learned how to smile hard enough so the corners of my eyes crinkled above my masks. I turned thirty. Ana turned twenty-five. Ava turned five. Milestone birthdays during a pandemic for everyone! Riley started school virtually, then shifted to a hybrid of in-person and virtual school, then completely in-person. He experienced a fresh kind of hell every day. We celebrated my thirtieth birthday by being very inebriated at home, which is the best way to celebrate turning thirty. We celebrated the holidays at our house. I learned the joy that is the vegan Celebration Roast, a store-bought lump that kind of looks like ham but is made of a combination of soy and vegetables. It looks disgusting and tastes delicious. Eating it was like securing the final Infinity Stone* to turn me into

---

* I promise never to make another *Avengers* reference ever again. This one just came to my mind, and it only felt right to include so you know who I really am: someone who, against all odds, does know who Thanos is and would kiss his large, purple face if given the opportunity.

That Person, who has a favorite flavor of LaCroix and talks about the moistness of a soy loaf.

At some point, I stopped trying to think too hard about how the pandemic was expanding the existing cracks in our society. The fact that schools function as a day care, a meal provider, counseling, and also have to make kids learn. The fact that nothing, not even a global pandemic, can stop billionaires from wealth hoarding. I will not write the specific amount of money Jeff Bezos earned last year, while Amazon delivery drivers were being overworked and underpaid. I will not write the amount because it would cause you to destroy this book in a fiery rage—understandably so—and you haven't even gotten to the part where I talk about my dog a lot.

Most concerningly, the pandemic further exposed the growing politicization of human decency. It's a problem that has permeated our culture for generations but a pandemic really let it rear its ugly, unmasked head. I got emails from family sharing videos purporting that the pandemic wasn't actually that big of a deal. I had conversations about the impact of isolation on mental health with people who have previously denied my depression. Why is it so hard to convince people to care about other people?

THE AFTER TIMES

I'm not sure if where we currently are, as I'm writing this, even classifies as the "after times." Maybe you, in the future, will laugh quietly to yourself, reminiscing like, "Ah, yes. Slowly making our way outdoors and weaning ourselves off face masks. I remember that. Seems like a lifetime ago." Or maybe there's a new virus variant and you're looking at this book through a hazmat suit. I'm not sure I fully believe that things are "getting back to normal" quite yet. And, if I'm being honest, if "normal" includes all the facets of where we were before I'm not sure I want to get back there at all.

How strange for the whole world to have collectively gone through this traumatic event and to just . . . keep going. For more than a year, we'd wake up every day knowing that a very scary thing was happening and the best thing we could do was literally nothing, to stay inside until it was safe to come out. It feels like the closest many of us got to acknowledging that was by simply saying, "This is pretty wild, huh?" and then we'd go back to answering emails and doing our jobs like it wasn't a health risk to leave the house. I know all the capitalist, work-until-you-die, rise-and-grind reasons why many of us were unable to stop, but that doesn't make it any less astonishing that we were never really given permission to stop, that we didn't feel allowed to stop.

Once Riley and I got fully vaccinated, we started doing things again. Remember doing things? Remember running to the store without following stickers to guide the flow of traffic so as to not have too many people in one aisle? Remember eating in restaurants without risking the livelihood of yourself and everyone around you? Remember having friends?

After more than a year spent almost entirely at home, my social stamina is at zero. I need a full day to recuperate from a happy hour. I have to remind myself people can see my face when I'm standing slack-jawed in the freezer aisle trying to figure out which ice cream won't make my farts entirely toxic. I wonder whether it will take a full year to regain the part of my personality that had any tolerance for small talk. I wonder whether that part will ever come back.

As I write this, we are on the precipice of summer. Hot vaxx summer! Thot girl summer! Time to rip off our masks and open-mouth kiss everyone we see! I plan to get slutty the best way I know how: drinking on restaurant patios with Riley and Ava. How foreign to make plans, to eat out, to return back to life as we knew it. Even getting back to normal feels a little bit strange and unprecedented.

LITTLE MISS SHITHEAD

I f you ever sat in a doctor's waiting room in the '90s, you probably encountered *Mr. Men* and *Little Miss* books. These series of children's books were meant to teach simple moral lessons through the mishaps and adventures of characters with names like Mr. Rude, Mr. Good, Little Miss Bad, and Little Miss Whoops. Mr. Rude learns that others don't like it when he yells at them or rips a huge fart. Mr. Good leaves his home of Badland where he is unappreciated for his goodness and goes to live in Goodland. The idea that there are "good" and "bad" places to live and the people who live there are inherently good or bad is, to put it politely, deeply fucked. Perhaps Little Miss Redlining could tell us more about that.

Most of the characters look how I imagine Pac-Man would appear straight on: a big circle head, tiny arms, and stumpy legs. Some have hats or hair accessories. Some have prominent noses or smiles. All are a single, specific trait personified—good, bad, naughty, talkative— and named as such. Most of the names are self-explanatory: Little Miss Bossy, Mr. Nosey, Little Miss Wise, Mr. Adventure. There is one named Mr. Tickle but I'm too scared to see what moral lesson he is meant to teach.

It's worth mentioning that many of the early Mr. Men appear to be adults while the Little Misses seem, at the oldest, like preteens. You can read into that as much or as little as you like.

In Little Miss Naughty's book, she goes around wreaking havoc on the misters in her world. She knocks off Mr. Uppity's hat. She breaks Mr. Clever's glasses. She pulls off Mr. Bump's bandages—his whole thing is that he's accident-prone, hence the bandages. The misters have a meeting to figure out how they're going to stop Little Miss Naughty and arrive at the brilliant idea to "tweak" her on the nose. Then, when she's about to do something naughty, she gets flicked on the nose and stops. That's it. That's the whole lesson.

Anyway, here's the story of one of the lost ladies from the series: Little Miss Shithead.

• •

Are you ever a shithead? Sometimes, I bet! Well, Little Miss Shithead was a shithead all the time.

On one particular Monday morning, she woke up and looked out the window. "Looks like a nice day," she said. "A nice day . . . to be a shithead!" The thought was so delicious to Little Miss Shithead that she decided to tweet it.

Within seconds, Little Miss Shithead had a notification. She smirked. Mr. Actually was in her mentions. "Actually," Mr. Actually replied, "this day isn't nice for everyone. Take me, for example. I had to wake up to a profane tweet from YOU. Back in my day, little misses didn't speak so crassly and needed their husband's permission to get a credit card. Perhaps you should think twice about what you say lest you ruin another person's day." Little Miss Shithead cocked her head at the response. Pausing a moment to look at Mr. Actually's profile picture—a sentient goatee with gas station sunglasses—Little Miss Shithead typed her reply: *fuck off :)*. Satisfied, she put on her signature yellow bow, smiled, and put her phone away.

She decided to walk to the café down the street and treat herself to a scone and some coffee. A delicious tweet deserved a delicious reward, she thought. Scone and coffee in hand, Little Miss Shithead left the café just as Mr. Ick was coming in. He held the door open for her and she said thanks. "How about a smile, too, miss?" Mr. Ick sneered. His upper lip curled uncomfortably toward his nose as if his own body were trying to escape the words he'd said. Little Miss Shithead looked at him, a twinkle in her eye. The corners of her mouth twitched for a moment, and then, without warning, Little Miss Shithead barfed a little. "What the hell?!" Mr. Ick cried, backing away to avoid the puke from soiling his shoes. "What's wrong with you?!" Little Miss Shithead smiled, wiped spittle from her mouth, and walked away. She took an extra big bite of her scone, feeling satisfied.

Little Miss Shithead made her way to the park to find a bench to enjoy the rest of her snack. As she sipped and ate, she looked up at the birds in the trees overhead, wondering what they might be chirping about and whether some birds were shitheads like her. "Lovely day," a voice said. Little Miss Shithead looked back down to see Mr. Meddlesome had taken the seat next to her. Little Miss Shithead finished the rest of her scone, nodded, and eyed all the unoccupied benches in her periphery. She took another sip of her coffee.

"Whatcha drinking?" Mr. Meddlesome gestured toward her cup, his finger nearly touching the lid. Little Miss Shithead pulled her cup away slightly. "Coffee," she replied and took another sip. "Ah," Mr. Meddlesome nodded. Little Miss Shithead turned her gaze back to the trees, watching one bird cheep at another. She thought to herself, *I wonder what they're*—"You waiting for your boyfriend or something?" Little Miss Shithead looked back at Mr. Meddlesome who was still staring at her. She shook her head no and turned her attention back to the birds and her coffee. She noticed one bird sitting alone on a branch and wondered, if she were to climb to a neighboring limb, whether it would support her weight. When Little Miss Shithead was younger, she used to climb a tree in the front yard of—

"So, are you Korean?" Little Miss Shithead slowly brought her cup of coffee to her mouth as Mr. Meddlesome kept talking. "I have a friend who's Korean and you remind me so much of her. Well, actually she's my dental hygienist . . ." As he talked, Little Miss Shithead kept the cup at her lips, letting the coffee softly glug out of the lid. Mr. Meddlesome didn't wait for a reply.

"She moved here when she was about your age, but her English has gotten pretty good since then. She told me her Korean name once but I forget how to say it. What's your name? I mean, your *real* name?" Little Miss Shithead continued pouring coffee into her mouth, which had become so full that brown liquid started dripping out of the corners of her lips. Mr. Meddlesome looked concerned. "Oops, it looks like you, uh, spilled a little," he said with a nervous laugh.

Little Miss Shithead just stared back at him. She kept the cup to her mouth, letting the *glug-glug-glug* of the coffee fill the silence. A steady stream of liquid was now pouring from her mouth, dripping down her chin and neck onto the bench. It was starting to pool. Mr. Meddlesome scootched away a bit. "Are you okay or . . . ?" He started to get up. Little Miss Shithead dumped the last drips of coffee into her mouth, her eyes now locked on his. She set the empty cup on the bench, nodded, and smiled widely as coffee and saliva spilled from behind her teeth. "Crazy bitch," Mr. Meddlesome muttered, and just as he stood, a big gloop of bird shit plopped on his head. As he scuffled away, Little Miss Shithead looked up to see the lone bird perched on the branch. She swore she saw it wink at her but thought that'd be too on the nose. With that, Little Miss Shithead wiped her mouth with her sleeve, threw away her coffee cup, and headed home.

Mr. Actually, Mr. Ick, and Mr. Meddlesome had a meeting on an anonymous message board. "Someone needs to teach Little Miss Shithead a lesson!" said Mr. Meddlesome. "Actually, yes! She must be stopped," Mr. Actually chimed in. The three misters thought and thought. "Maybe we could dox her?" Mr. Ick suggested. The two misters paused before deciding that punishment didn't fit the crime. "That's too soft," Mr. Meddlesome said. "We need something that'll really make her think twice before she behaves this way again." "We could punch her in the face?" Mr. Ick said. ". . . I mean, ha ha, JK, we shouldn't do that." The other misters agreed half-heartedly. Mr. Actually googled "ways to punish little misses worse than being doxxed but not as bad as punching" and was redirected to articles about little misses talking about the consequences of misters knowing their addresses. "Actually," he began, "anything we do will just give her more attention and obviously she just wants attention."

"Well, if it's attention she wants, why don't we just ignore her?" Mr. Actually, Mr. Ick, and Mr. Meddlesome considered the suggestion. "That could actually work," Mr. Actually said. "So, it's settled," Mr. Meddlesome replied. "We ignore her. At least for the rest of the week." The three misters logged off, reveling in their genius.

Little did they know the suggestion came from a certain little shithead who'd managed to sneak onto the misters' message board. (It wasn't hard. It was a public forum.) Little Miss Shithead smirked quietly to herself, thinking about all the ways she could be a shithead without any misters getting in her way. She could tweet with reckless abandon, sip on coffee in the park, look at the birds until the sun went down. Her smile faded a bit. None of those things sounded particularly shithead-y. She thought harder, trying to remember all the ways she'd been a shithead in the past, hoping to find something shitty to do while the misters let her be.

There was the time she didn't laugh at Mr. Improv's bit about how gross periods are. She couldn't remember the punch line but did recall him flinging the mic around like his dick for three full minutes. There was the time she didn't message Mr. DM back even though he'd asked how her day was *before* requesting toe pics. (Little Miss Shithead doesn't even have toes.) Once, she swore she caught Mr. Ick smelling her hair and said, "Did you just smell my hair?" Mr. Ick, near tears, started talking about how he was bullied in middle school for how he smelled and how shitty it was for her to bring that up.

Little Miss Shithead tried to remember the very first time she was a shithead. Maybe it was in elementary school when a young mister whose name escapes her now said that only ugly little misses wore their hair "like that." (Little Miss Shithead is drawn bald.) Maybe it was when she told Miss Teacher and Miss Teacher said that tattling wasn't very nice. Maybe when she was a baby she cried in a shitty way? *Is Shithead my first or last name?* she wondered.

Little Miss Shithead would never remember the first time she acted like a shithead. She would never find out if she inherited her shittiness at birth or if it was bestowed upon her by some higher Miss or Mister. She would spend the next week getting coffee and going to the park, staring at birds in the trees, wondering which ones were shitheads, which were meddlesome, which were good and rude and funny and clumsy.

On Friday, she'd notice one bird adding a small yellow string to its nest. The bird would notice her back and exchange what she'd swear was a knowing look. Then, the bird would fly away. Little Miss Shithead would sit there a little while longer, eventually saying to herself, "What a nice day."

THINGS THAT ARE SO BAD THEY'RE GOOD

Sleeping until noon
Picking a pimple
Beer that's so sour it's kind of barfy
Fresh Parmesan cheese
The way the hyenas from *The Lion King* just are
Plucking a rogue body hair
Biting a ball of aluminum foil
How Sharpies smell
How Warheads taste
Ava, when she does a sad walk to her kennel after barking with the combined volume of every small dog that has ever existed
Most food puns
Closed caption descriptions for actions with modifiers (e.g., walks depressingly, sighs hornily)
Holding your pee for too long and then trying to go pee but you can't at first and you panic that it went back up in your body and got . . . stuck? But then you pee a bunch.
The entire *Love Island* franchise
Peeing in the shower

When you think you got your period but it's just the usual goop

Most things produced by our bodies

"Butterfly" by Crazy Town

The Purge

Swiping through your little sister's Tinder

Finding a loose piece of produce in a place you don't expect, like an orange rolling around a parking structure or a head of cabbage in the gutter

Comic Sans

Screaming as loud as you can in the car

McDonald's french fries

Eating one bite too many

Faking sick, and then getting away with it

Bioré pore strips

The background vocals of every song in a Mary-Kate and Ashley movie, where preteens are lip-synching lyrics very obviously sung by fully grown women

Dropping a glass—the cleanup is bad and accidentally breaking something sucks but there is always a brief moment after I hear glass shatter that my body goes "hell yeah"

ASMR videos

When an important person farts and they continue like nothing happened

This one Vine where a kid is running and an adult asks, "Let me see what you have." and the kid yells, "A KNIFE!" with such chaotic glee it's palpable

When you can tell a scene in a movie is using a body double

Remembering Trix yogurt

Finding out someone dislikes the same person as you

Cutting off a chunk of your own hair

SHE'S NICE THOUGH

Giving someone the finger
Cracking your knuckles
Those photo sets of croissants where one is actually a dog curled up
Every picture I took on a disposable camera during high school
Other people falling really hard but not getting hurt
My brain

SCARY STORIES TO KEEP YOU UP AT NIGHT

On a mild and partly cloudy day, a young woman walked into a coffee shop. When she got to the register, she said, "One oat milk latte." A slight shudder ran down her back at her own nonchalance while asking for nondairy milk in public. The cashier asked for her name and she said "Mia." The cashier handed her a receipt and said, "All right, Nia, we'll call out your name when it's ready." She almost corrected the cashier, but thankfully remembered the horror stories from friends who'd made that mistake before. ("It was so bad! I was like, *No, it's with a P as in 'Puddle of Mudd.'* Then, they started talking to me about '90s alt bands. I don't know why I made that pull—I don't think I've ever even listened to Puddle of Mudd!") She spent so long thinking about the "Puddle of Mudd" thing that her latte was ready by the time she snapped out of it. She took the drink back to her table.

She put her earbuds in, took a sip of her latte, double-checked that her earbuds were actually plugged in, and resumed listening to her podcast about a serial killer whose calling card was eating his victims' hair. She pulled an earbud out to triple-check that they weren't half in, half out—it's happened before and now she can never return to that library. "Oh, I think she grabbed it by mistake," she heard the cashier say. She looked up and realized they'd gestured toward her. The cashier continued, "I'll make you a new one."

She broke out in a cold sweat and the room got blurry. She had committed the most heinous offense: she'd taken someone else's coffee accidentally. She knew she had to leave; the authorities were probably already on the way. She gathered her things and tried to discreetly rush out the door. As she stepped outside, she felt a pang in her chest so sharp it stopped her in her tracks: she realized she had forgotten to say thank you.

● ●

A car beeps at you and you don't know what you did wrong. You spend the rest of the drive so consumed by the idea you offended another driver you don't realize your blinker has been on this whole time. Your car is so embarrassed for you that when you get home, it dies.

● ●

You and your husband are sitting on the couch, unwinding after a long day. It's a standard nighttime ritual, but something seems . . . off. "What do you want to watch?" you ask. "There's a new documentary on Roth IRAs we could try," he says. You're taken aback. "What?" he asks. "Nothing," you reply. "It's just . . . usually I ask what you want to watch and you say, 'I don't know, what do you want to watch?' and we go back and forth like that for fifteen minutes before inevitably watching an old episode of *The O.C.*" "Oh, we can watch *The O.C.*," he says but you tell him the Roth IRA documentary is fine. (It's not, but you're going to spend the whole time staring at your phone regardless.)

The second the opening credits start, you get up to go to the bathroom, where you'll pretend to pee and watch TikToks for thirty-five minutes. "I'll pause it," he says. "No, it's fine," you say on your way to the bathroom. "It's just the opening credits." "Yeah, but I don't want you to miss anything," he says. "No, no. Don't wait on my behalf," you yell from the toilet. "Okay," he yells back, "I'll keep it paused just in case." *In case of what*, you wonder, but not for too long, because the longer you stay in here the longer the movie is paused and the longer before the movie is over and you can watch TikToks instead.

You return to the couch where your husband is waiting patiently. His phone is nowhere in sight. He's just sitting there, waiting for you. "Are you okay?" you ask. "Yes," he says and seems like he means it. He unpauses the movie and you start scrolling through Instagram.

"Do you want me to pause again?" he asks. "No, it's good. It's easier for me to pay attention when I'm doing two things at once," you lie. "Are you lying?" he asks. ". . . Yeah?" you say, confused why he also isn't playing a game on his phone. He hasn't touched his phone at all. Wait . . . his phone isn't even in the room. Who watches a movie without staring at their phone the whole time?! Finally, it clicks.

"Hold on, is this—"

"Yep, you're dead, and this is hell."

"Ah, that makes sense. When I tried to pee nothing came out and I was like, 'Oh god, do I have a UTI?' but it was probably just on account of being dead. Okay, well, you can press play, I guess."

• •

I awoke to a CRASH in the middle of the night. Turns out my shower curtain had fallen because I did a bad job putting up the tension rod.

• •

Ruth awoke one morning with a small red spot on her face. At first, she couldn't remember if she'd always had the spot or if the spot showed up overnight. But once she noticed the spot, it was all she could think about. Throughout the day, she ran her finger across the spot, trying to see if it was getting bigger and turning into a bump. Eventually, she remembered hearing that touching her face would give her pimples so she tried to limit how much she poked and prodded. I mean, she already had the one spot to deal with.

She soon realized the spot was definitely getting bigger. By the next morning, it had become a full-on boil. It was red and tender, and Ruth was sure it was something bad. "It'll go away, just don't scratch it," her mom told her over the phone. When Ruth hung up, she immediately went to WebMD's symptom checker. Scratching at her face, she typed in "bump." She scrolled through all the autofilled options—bump on butt, widespread purplish bump, single crusty pus-filled bump—until she found one that fit. She clicked "continue" and steeled herself for the onslaught of horrors. Shingles, scabies, hand-foot-and-mouth disease, Grover's disease. The latter was most common among middle-aged men but Ruth didn't want to take her chances. She made a doctor's appointment for that afternoon.

"So," the doctor began, after checking the bump, "I don't want you to panic but . . ." Ruth immediately started to panic. She wondered how long she had left. Would she be able to visit her family? Would she have time to get through her bucket list? Would she have time to tidy her house up a bit before distant relatives came over? Would she have time to make a bucket list and then do even one of the things on the list? "It appears that a spider has laid eggs in your face," the doctor said.

"Oh, thank god," Ruth sighed. "I thought it was cancer or something." Ruth went home, excited that she'd soon be a mother.

PART 2

Yellow Fever

Yellow Fever

NICE GIRLS
FINISH EVENTUALLY

The first time I kissed someone I didn't like, I was nine-teen. A guy from my creative writing class asked me to get coffee and I was like, "Yay! A friend!" And then, after coffee, we went to the grocery store and got stuff to make tacos and I was like, "Wow! A friend who likes to cook!" We went back to his house, made and ate the tacos, and I was like, "It's cool for the first time you hang out with a new friend to last three or four hours, right?" After dinner, his hot roommate came home, and I thought, *Oh dang, maybe I should have eaten, like, one less taco just in case, you know?* But it wasn't until the hot roommate, upon seeing us sitting on the couch, was like, "Well . . . I'll leave you two aLoNe" that I realized, *Oh. This has been a date the whole time, hasn't it?*

At that point, I began to notice the lulls in conversation, the way he'd turned himself to face me. My classmate asked why I was sitting so far away. I'd been seated at the opposite side of the couch, which didn't seem "so far away," but I'd also been measuring in platonic distances. I responded with something like, "Hah, I don't know," which was a lie but seemed kinder than the truth.

When he asked if I wanted to cuddle—yes, literally said the words, "Do you want to cuddle?"—I felt my vagina retract farther up

51

inside of me. But he had asked, and did so nicely, so I scooted within his reach. As he put his arm around me, I wondered why I was still there, why I hadn't left earlier when there'd been that lull in our conversation or as soon as he started talking about how girls told him he looked hot with a ponytail. His hair *was* objectively beautiful. It was long, shiny, and curly, like how I imagined mine would've looked if the perm my mom gave me in fourth grade had turned out right. I remember thinking I shouldn't compliment his hair as that would insinuate I was into him and, on the very unlikely chance that this was, oh, I don't know, a date, I didn't want to lead him on. Then, I proceeded to hang out and talk with him for another full hour.

In my defense, I hadn't been on many (any?) dates up to that point. Casual dating in middle school meant looking longingly at a guy three seats behind me when the teacher gave me a stack of papers and told me to "take one and pass it back." Casual dating in high school meant rerouting the way I walked during passing periods so I would briefly brush shoulders with him in the hall. If we were getting serious, I might have even said "hi." At nineteen, I didn't know what casual dating in college was supposed to look like. I assumed it'd be different from dating in middle and high school but I wasn't sure how. I hoped it'd be more than just making out during the end credits of *Garden State* in my parents' basement one time or having friends ask other friends if the friend that I liked liked anyone and if that "anyone" was me. I assumed, when the situation arose, I'd figure it out.

In my classmate's defense, we had absolutely been on a date. If someone had recounted the entirety of this interaction back to me— he asked me out, we got to know each other over coffee, he asked if I wanted to have dinner, we went grocery shopping together, we went back to his place, made dinner, kept talking—and asked, "Is that a date?," I would say, "Duh, obviously." After he put his arm around my shoulder, he asked if he could kiss me and I remember thinking, *It'd be mean if I said no.*

My sister Ana and I often do a sort of group therapy with each other where we laugh and scream about the people we've hooked up with to varying degrees just because we "felt bad" and didn't want to hurt their feelings. To be clear, while some of these incidents do have overlapping elements with more insidious and illegal violations of boundaries, they are not one and the same. I feel lucky that I've never been made to feel scared or in danger, and I'm sad and angry and embarrassed that my reaction to not ever having been assaulted is "I'm lucky."

The space between a mutual sexual encounter and one that is nonconsensual is littered with a lot of "at leasts." Sure, I danced with a guy I didn't want to at that bar, but at least it made him leave me alone. Yeah, I let my Tinder date kiss me good night even though he reminded me of someone I babysat. At least that was all he asked to do. When my classmate who was kind and funny and fun to hang out with asked if he could kiss me, I said okay because I thought it'd be rude to tell him no. So, I leaned in and, though it made me like myself a little less, I thought, *At least he won't think I'm mean.*

In my mind, a casual acquaintance thinking I was mean was somehow worse than existing in a state of cognitive dissonance in which I did date-like things with that acquaintance while convincing myself that he, like me, did not think this was a date. I figured it was polite to go along with whatever he wanted to do as long as he asked nicely, which he did, so really we were both just minding our manners.

To be clear, he didn't dramatically misread the situation. I didn't decline when he wanted to sit closer. After I said he could kiss me, I didn't lean away or say that I didn't think of him that way or slide onto the floor and become a pile of plasma waiting to be absorbed by the carpet. I am so cowardly when it comes to confrontation, so terrified of people I barely know thinking I'm rude or unlikable, that I will make small concessions with my body like it is a restaurant and I don't want a bad Yelp review. *Dinner included a nicely cut avocado. Kinda made mouth into a butthole shape when we kissed but did let me kiss. 3.5/5 stars.*

If you're related to me, you can stop reading now. The essay ends here for you because I'm about to talk about sex things. You get to make what you will of the fact that I regret kissing people I didn't really want to. Maybe make up a fun conclusion where I travel back in time to interrupt Past Me moments before each kiss. Maybe have me call myself on my old Nokia, like, *Hi, I'm you from the future. I don't have time to explain, but maybe go home now.* I wonder if that would've fucked me up less.

Now, for all who are *not* my family members: From the very first time I had sex, it took me well over a year to have orgasm. I'd had one before, sans partner, so I knew what was missing, but my dissatisfaction didn't register as a tragedy or even a problem to solve. I was in a long-term, monogamous relationship so I couldn't chalk it up to bad one-night stands or it being too early in a relationship to be, like, "oopsie, wrong button." I knew that what I was experiencing—or, I guess, wasn't experiencing—was common, and, rather than take that as a sign of a greater issue, I assumed it was par for the course, just something I should go along with. All this to say that I remember feeling like faking it would be the nice thing to do. Like, it'd be mean if I didn't cum.

The reasons I faked it are boring and what you'd expect: it was taking a long time, I worried my partner at the time was getting annoyed or bored or grossed out even though he never expressed any of those things, and I'd do it quicker on my own later. I remember him being hurt when I eventually did have an orgasm and, in my excitement, blurted out that it was the first time that'd happened with him. We were celebrating a marathon he didn't realize we'd been running for over a year. It'd been me at the starting line, the finish line, and on the route with signs that said, MAYBE NEXT TIME! and A LITTLE LOWER! I didn't realize that what I thought was protecting his feelings was in fact a year of being dishonest. In trying to preserve some imagined version of his pride, I ended up hurting him more.

It's a gross oversimplification to say that sexism is the sole reason I missed out on a year's worth of orgasms—it's also not true, a dibble dabble of self-hatred and self-consciousness are also to blame—but the two aren't unrelated. Somewhere along the way, I've absorbed the notion that pleasure is optional for me. That saying what I do or don't want is mean. That I must swallow my discomfort to preserve the comfort of the men around me.

I am too bored by the idea that "nice guys finish last" to give it any more space than this sentence. I think it's far more damaging to be gracious to men who've been told kindness to women is not a requirement of, say, dating women, but is a trait that should be immediately rewarded. Niceness as transaction. The nice guy moves over and makes room for you on flights, trains, and Ubers, but probably still needs to be asked in order to do so. He listens or at least looks like he's listening. He's chivalrous—you'll know because he'll tell you. He doesn't always think of himself first—he's still thinking of himself, just not first. He is often doing the bare minimum when it comes to, not just romantic relationships, but any relationship. I mean, he doesn't regularly ask his *friends* how they are. And look! He held a door! Or said "thanks" to a waiter! Or acknowledged your feelings once! Of course, not feelings like "I think we'd be better as friends" or "I'm not interested in dating you." But why would you turn down a Nice Guy?? What more could you want from a partner than someone who will do the dishes when you remind him to do the dishes? What could be better than a relationship where goodness is transactional? Where men's kindness is an achievement and women's bodies are an earned congratulations?

Meanwhile, I'm doling out parts of my body like they're each a consolation prize. Sorry, you can't have all of me, just the parts you ask for politely. Nice girls do what they are told. Above all, nice girls don't make things uncomfortable or unpleasant.

A few years ago, I was home visiting my family and saw the guy from my creative writing class at a coffee shop. I was waiting for my drink when I noticed him in a corner booth with a few other people. His hair was in a ponytail. I didn't go say "hi," obviously—do you know me at all?

I don't think he noticed me or if he did, even remembered me, which was a relief and, in the moment, maybe a tiny bit of a disappointment.

Would I prefer to be remembered as mean, or be nice, and be forgotten entirely?

WHAT DOES IT MEAN WHEN A GIRL IS QUIET?

Quiet girls have long been a mystery to men and to the world itself—and did I mention to men? What does it mean when a girl is being quiet around you, not verbally acknowledging your presence? What is she trying to say by not talking to you at all? After decades of research and absolutely zero conversations with women, we finally have some answers.

When a girl is quiet, it's because she has a million things on her mind. She is trying to envision one million different things. Bicycle, bag of chips, a dog dressed to look like a cat and vice versa. You should ask if she wants help thinking of more things.

When a girl is being very quiet, it's because she's eavesdropping on another conversation. How interesting! You should tell her she's so interesting.

When a girl is extra quiet, it could mean she is mad. It could also mean she is sad. Perhaps she is glad or even thinking about Brad, that kid in elementary school who already had abs somehow. Her silence could be an expression of any of these rhyming things, but it's probably the Brad one.

When a girl is quiet, she's concentrating on holding in a fart.

When she is loud, it is to conceal a fart. A girl is always farting or about to fart.

When a girl is quite, she just made a typo.

A shy girl is sometimes a quiet girl. But a quiet girl isn't always shy. It's kind of like how all squares are rectangles, but not all rectangles are squares. Do architects design a building and go, "I made this room a square and, in turn, it is also a rectangle," and the construction team is like, "Excellent, this changes everything"? A quiet girl is like that.

When a girl isn't saying anything, it's fine because a man will always say the thing she's about to say, only louder.

When a girl isn't smiling, watch out! She could be about to explode. A quiet, nonsmiling girl is a ticking time bomb. Oh, wait—this one isn't a girl at all but a literal bomb. The ticking sound should have given it away. It did seem weird that she had no skin and was made of wires. Seemed rude to ask, though, because girls can be so sensitive. Or is that bombs? I always confuse the two.

When a girl isn't saying much, it's probably just the first half of this movie. Once the male protagonist solves her murder and avenges her rape, she will say three or even four lines in a flashback.

When a girl is wearing headphones in public, she is probably waiting for you to ask what she is listening to. In fact, it would be rude not to ask. Why else does someone have headphones on in public if not to invite conversation?

A quiet girl reading a book is the loudest kind of quiet girl.

When a girl is quiet, she's probably thinking about how good you are at talking.

Quiet girls are complicated. Loud girls are complicated, too. All girls are complicated because if you talk to them in person, then they might respond with their own thoughts, feelings, expectations, etc. And that just gets too hard to follow.

A quiet girl is the kind of girl you want to take home to your mom. Your mom is also a quiet girl. The two of them will get along well, just shrugging and nodding silently back and forth at each other. Now that you think about it, all the girls in your life are quiet. Maybe it's because you're really loud? You've never heard a quiet girl finish a sentence, so you guess that means they can't? You're really good at finishing sentences, so you're being helpful when you finish theirs for them. Which is also a solid way to flirt, you think.

Loud girls are scary to me. It's, like, why are you talking at full volume and typing using all caps? That's just unnecessary and very masculine.

When a girl isn't talking, it might mean she just doesn't want to talk to you right now. It seems too obvious, but it's SOMETIMES TRUE!

When a boy is quiet, especially around women, that makes him a feminist and that's really brave of him.

Either that, or he's thinking about rectangles.

HOW TO WIFE

*H*usband is a terrible word. It's one that feels bad to say and, in conversation, always seems like a threat. *I don't know if we require your services, Door-to-Door Bug Exterminator. Let me ask my* HUSBAND. It can be shortened to *hubby*, an equally terrible word that makes me think of elementary school cubbies. This then makes me think about how the smells of pencil shavings and cafeterias, when combined, are akin to vomit. Used as a verb, *husband* means "to manage carefully" à la animal husbandry, a phrase that surprisingly has nothing to do with marrying a horse. Etymologically speaking, the word sucks. I would much rather have a wife.

Wife implies softness and servitude and a maternal-adjacent love, which I know is gross but tell me it's not true. It is a setup (take my wife . . . please!) and a punch line (winks in *Borat*). The word feels warm and welcoming and is made better by the fact that it rhymes with *knife*. *Wife* sounds like a summer breeze and smells like a subtle hint of vanilla. It's Julianne Moore rubbing my back until I fall asleep.

Asian wife is its own thing altogether, specifically an Asian wife of a white husband. To be an Asian wife means you get to go to restaurants, parks, and grocery stores and have old men you do not know tell your husband how lucky he is to be with someone "so exotic." You'll be told this is a compliment, so you smile in a way that implies "thank you" without having to lie out loud. You get to meet extended family, who will also look to your husband, nod at you, and go, "Wow, so pretty!" If asked to describe your face beyond "kinda Asian, I guess?" they'd pause and try to decide which of the three racially ambiguous actors they could compare you to. They'll always settle on Olivia Munn, which you'll also be told is a compliment. You'll get to think about how your children—you're going to have kids, right? Right?!—will be whiter than you and wonder whether that, in turn, will make you look more Asian or less. You'll get to watch the kids live, laugh, love, and grow up to marry Asian wives or become Asian wives. Or, I guess, Asian-ish wives.

Is now a good time to say I've been married to my husband, Riley, for three years? This somehow feels like a hundred years and like two months, and I mean both as a compliment. Though, technically and legally speaking, he is my husband, he deserves a better, more appropriate title. Like Boyfriend Super Plus or Mr. Mia Mercado. I love being married to him and telling people that we're married. I hate saying that he's my husband.

Having a wife sounds great. However, *being* a wife? No, thanks. Wifedom comes with too shitty a history and far too many rules: look hot always, make dinner every night, be a constant vessel for Husband's Seed, don't complain too often, don't menstruate too loudly, shiny hair, natural makeup, vacuum in Victorian dresses, cook in a corset, forget how to read, etc. Hard pass. I'd rather be a husband.

Husbands get to come home from Big Job and eat hunk of meat, loosen their belt, and watch TV until they fall asleep with a glass of whiskey in their hand. Do I enjoy whiskey? Not particularly, but it's a sacrifice I'd happily make if it means I never ever have to shimmy my shoulders and whisper *I'm so bad* anytime I think about eating dessert. Historically, Husband is a role that's merely a single facet of someone rather than an all-consuming identity. Why else would the *Real Househusbands* series never have taken off like its female counterpart?

Of course, this is not at all what modern marriage looks like. That involves divvying up your various streaming subscription fees and showing each other parts of the internet until you fall asleep. It's asking where the other wants to eat until you die. It's me watching *Gossip Girl* on Netflix while Riley sells turnips on *Animal Crossing*, both of us explaining to the other the intricacies of our respective worlds. He guides me on a tour of the exact replica he's created of our house in this village run by a raccoon. I treat him, once again, to live commentary on the scene in season three, episode ten where Hilary Duff talk-sings Lady Gaga's "LoveGame" while playing Snow White. (I'd give more context but that'd just confuse you more.) It's watching a twenty-minute tutorial on how to solve Cryptic Crosswords, a genre of word puzzles exclusively by dorks for dorks. Sure, sex is great, but have you ever perfectly completed the *New York Times* crossword ninety-five days in a row?

However, a hearty LO-fucken-L if you think modern marriage is completely divorced from all its archaic connotations. There's a reason I told the Bug Guy I'd "ask my husband" if we required an exterminator, and there's a reason why it worked as a means to get him to leave.

There's this one podcast episode I think about sometimes—don't worry, I'm not going to talk at length about a podcast lest we both pass away. The podcast, *Where Should We Begin?*, is hosted by psychotherapist and relationship expert Esther Perel. If you've ever wanted to reflect on your own relationships and eavesdrop on other people's therapy sessions—I don't understand a person who isn't even a tiny bit interested in doing the latter—I highly recommend it. The particular episode I think about is a session with a husband and wife exploring an open relationship. Specifically, the wife wants to have romantic relationships with other women and wonders what that means about herself, her sexuality, and her marriage. In their conversation, Perel posits that, at its core, it sounds like what the wife is drawn to is eroticism from reciprocated emotional intimacy. She says that, maybe, what the wife sought was a Wife of her own.

This is a gross oversimplification of the episode, which has a more nuanced take on the open relationship and intimacy as a whole. But a wife wanting a Wife, in a very cishet way, feels so culturally familiar. It sounds like period dramas where a handmaiden and their Lady have long, seaside conversations about who they are and who they've been. Their hair blows in the salty breeze and they look at each other like, *What if we . . . kissed?* (They close mouthed kiss for two seconds in the climax of the film.) It looks like novels-turned-movies in which a Lonely Housewife develops a deep level of emotional intimacy with her hot female friend after being listened to for one (1) entire conversation. They don't end up together but the encounter leaves the housewife emboldened enough to show her husband where the clitoris is. Feminism win!

Plus, wives are maids you get to marry! Wives are mothers you get to fuck! It's not funny to joke about asking your husband for permission to do something. But asking your wife? A riot! Put it on novelty mugs and Facebook memes! For this reason, nothing makes me nauseous like an overprotective man. The line between protection and ownership is blurred by years of female servitude and T-shirts that say things like, I'M A DAD WITH DAUGHTERS AND A GUN TO SHOOT YOUR NUTS OFF.

There was no conversation where my dad "gave his blessing" to Riley prior to our wedding, specifically because I didn't want there to be. There are plenty of good reasons for a parent and their future child-in-law to talk before upcoming nuptials—to impart advice, to become more acquainted, to practice those handshakes where you bring the other person in for a hug and pat them on the back. But Riley and I didn't have any reasons that didn't ultimately boil down to vague obligation. We did talk to both my parents and both his parents about getting married before getting engaged. This was almost exclusively in the spirit of sharing news we were excited about and asking them to please clap. I'm grateful those conversations didn't feel like asking a teacher to go to the bathroom, waiting to be corrected for saying *can I* instead of *may I.*

Aside from getting on his health insurance and sometimes receiving mail addressed to Mrs. Riley Taylor—who is she?—getting married hasn't changed our relationship significantly. At least not any more than a relationship changes based on things like time, life experience, and being quarantined in a global pandemic. As we've well surpassed the ten-thousand-hour mark of being together, I would consider myself an expert on our relationship. Thus, I will impart unto you something we've employed to maintain a happy, healthy marriage: create shorthand phrases that would confuse or concern others. For example:

- "Should we do our stuff?" is something Riley and I started saying during quarantine that I think will continue until we die. These five words connote the following series of events: Riley makes coffee, we start doing the daily crossword, I leave halfway through to poop, I come back and Riley says that was too short a time for me to have pooped (it's not). Once we finish the crossword, we do the Spelling Bee, a different *New York Times* daily word game that involves finding anagrams from a jumble of letters and asking, "Okay, 'doodoo' didn't work, but do you think the *Times* accepts 'peepee' as a word?"
- (They don't.)

- "Do you want to have a nasty boy dinner?" translates to "We're out of something in bulk like toilet paper, sparkling water, or the breakfast cereal Riley has eaten literally every day for seven years. (Help!) Want to go to Costco and get a hot dog?"
- "Do you see my son?" is a recurring chorus in our household. It means, "Our dog, Ava, who is female, is doing something cute, stupid, gross, weird, embarrassing, or all of the above." We call Ava our son because shortly after we got her, we took her to a PetSmart to get various dog necessities like a collar that doesn't have leopard print like her previous one did and fifteen boxes of dog treats. While Riley and I were staring at boxes of treats, trying to figure out which wouldn't make her farts smell even worse, a person, at the end of the aisle shouted, "UM . . . HE'S POOPING." We turned to see Ava taking a shit in the middle of the PetSmart aisle, looking up at us like, "Mother, Father, I am sorry for my sin." When Ava poops, she looks like Mr. Burns from *The Simpsons*: hunched in a way that seems physically impossible, somehow both lanky and small, head too big for her body. From then on, Riley and I have exclusively referred to Ava as our son, our terrible little child who shits wherever she pleases.
- "Oh . . . *bebe*" in a regretful tone means "Mia, your morning breath is rancid. Go do something about that before it kills us both."

Another secret to our marriage is disagreeing about inconsequential things. He thinks raw unsalted almonds are an enjoyable snack. I know that is the reason why, were I to murder him, the courts would rule it as self-defense. He refuses to admit it is fine to pee in the shower. I refuse to let him tell me anything more about the intricacies of LEGO building. (He just told me LEGO is "technically all caps." *That* will actually be the reason courts deem his death "understandable.") Learning how to disagree without resorting to rage or resulting in homicide is a lot easier when the subject is "Are wraps sandwiches or burritos? Discuss."

At one point in that episode of *Where Should We Begin?*, Perel suggests that "what we long for in romantic love is to be unique, indispensable, and irreplaceable to at least one person." Maybe that's why titles like Husband and Wife don't feel fitting to me. The implication that we are filling some predetermined role seems gross. It doesn't encompass the unique and specific ways we've learned how the other feels loved, appreciated, heard, and supported. For him, it's words of affirmation and sharing music he's made that is far over my head. For me, it's rewatching Hilary Duff sing that song in *Gossip Girl.* I suppose we are learning less about how to be a wife or a husband and more about how to be ourselves with each other.

YELLOW FEVER

desperately want people to think I am hot, which is the most embarrassing thing I've ever written down.

I know it's ugly to want to be seen as hot. You shouldn't want to be hot! You're perfect just the way you are, you lumpy slug! It shouldn't matter whether other people find you attractive because it's what's on the inside that counts. And technically, your blackheads are *inside* your pores so would it kill you to do one of those face masks that sucks your soul out of your face? Could you do it once or twice or every other day for the rest of your life? Okay, but what if we call it "self-care"?

Desirability is a conundrum. Sometimes, all I want is for every person who has ever lived to tell me I am gorgeous. Other times, I feel like if I am in any way observed, I will commit arson. I want the freedom to look hot without anyone saying anything about it, except maybe in the comments section and only with fire emojis. I crave the knowledge that I am seen without anyone actually looking at me and saying, "I see you."

Once, when I still worked in a corporate office, I came back from a work photo shoot in full glam, or as glam as a stuffy corporate photo shoot can get. I liked how I looked and liking how I look makes me feel better about myself. I know that is superficial and shallow, but as I spend most of my waking hours thinking about things that make me feel worse about myself—like whether or not I'm doing my taxes correctly—I refuse to write glam off just yet as a potential solution to all my problems.

On the long trek from the parking garage to my cubicle, I mentally put the first thirty seconds of Beyoncé's "Crazy in Love" on repeat, one of the most struttable intros even if said strutting is only done in your head. I imagined doing a hair flip so devastating it teleported me back to my fart-soaked office chair. I wondered how glamorous you need to look before you can stop doing normie stuff like "work." I hoped the hugeness of my fake eyelashes was enough to distract from my growing pit stains.

Any semblance of self-confidence I'd mustered quickly shriveled up when I got back to my desk and multiple men I worked with—I think the correct number is "a gross"—forgot how to act. One coworker couldn't stop talking about the "stuff" on my face, probably aware that any qualitative statement would be inappropriate but unable to simply say nothing. Another jokingly asked me to prom. He'd started working at the company years before I had my first period. I'd never felt so naked and overdressed at the same time.

I know I would have been a tiny bit disappointed had none of my coworkers reacted to my itty-bitty makeover. It is a strange and humiliating kind of devastation to feel like you look good in public and have the public respond with resounding silence. Still, I'm not sure that would have been worse than feeling my coworkers' sweaty eyes on me while I turned back to my laptop and tried to respond to emails. After a little while, I took my eyelashes off in the bathroom and shoved them in my pocket.

After work, in an effort to gas me up, a friend texted me to ask, "What did [boyfriend at the time] say about your makeup when you got home?!?" I realized he hadn't said anything. So, I looked at him, loudly batted my reapplied, slightly crumpled lashes, like, "Notice anything *blink blink* *different*?" He was like, "Oh, you're wearing makeup." I know this can be read with sweet intentions. His lack of reaction could have implied that he found me attractive all the time; the massive lashes and contour were merely details he hadn't noticed. It's like feminist scholar Drake once said: "Sweatpants, hair tied, chillin' with no make-up on / That's when you're the prettiest, I hope that you don't take it wrong."

I know I would have felt offended in an opposite but equal way had he been like, "Hello, Hot Version of Girlfriend. What a pleasant surprise! You are so much hotter than Regular Girlfriend. Will you stay, please?" But when he looked at my painted face and remained mostly unmoved, I felt like a kid who had put on their mom's shoes and everyone at the dinner party reacted like, "Aw, look at the little lady! Hello, little lady!" It's a quiet mix of disappointment and humiliation to feel like you look good in private and have your partner say nothing.

When I was in college, I remember a woman who had been with her husband for a couple decades telling me that once you get married, you just stop caring about whether other people find you attractive. Maybe it was a command and not a commentary on the inevitable: just *stop caring* about whether people find you attractive. I am very much married and, to reiterate my humiliating admission, I still very much care whether other people think I'm hot.

Beauty is cultural currency—this is nothing new. I know it's instinctive to pay attention to a person you think is attractive. I know the actor portrayal in the movie is almost always hotter than the actual person. I know billions of dollars are made off us pulling and squeezing and smoothing and looking as small and young and white-passing as science and Gwyneth Paltrow make possible. (The hottest age to be is your age cut in half, minus an additional seven years.) And I know that all that sucks, but I still want to feel like I have a full bank account of an ass.

Like most every other part of my life, my physical self-image is heavily—okay, entirely—derived from external validation. I ask Riley how I look nearly every time we leave the house, and then I ask him thrice more, ignore him each time, and eventually say, "You're lying to be nice!" On more than one occasion, Riley has ended my fun little "ugly or pretty??" game by asking something along the lines of, "Is anything I say actually going to impact the way you feel about yourself?" And I said, "Yes, but only if you tell me I look bad."

My need for external validation is further complicated by the fact that I don't know how to feel sexy without also feeling sexualized. I don't believe my husband when he says I look okay, but I absolutely don't want my male coworkers to imply they like how I look. When Riley says I look okay, I don't believe him because, like a mother or an enchanted mirror, he *has* to say that. If he doesn't, our marriage just automatically gets annulled. But when a man I don't have any relationship with comments on the way I look, it feels more sinister than sweet. It feels like a threat, an implication of his browser history, a reminder that the way I look comes with a preamble of sexual connotations I cannot control.

Asian women, like children or decorations, are meant to be seen, not heard. We are sexy and submissive, sexy *because* we are submissive. We are exotic and unthreatening, eager to please without reciprocation. I should take it as a *compliment* that the bulk of my on-screen representation has been in pornographic subcategories. I should feel *flattered* that all I need to do is exist for someone to objectify me.

I don't need to recant the chorus of microaggressions that rings in the back of my head for you to imagine the things people have said to me, about me, about people who look like me. You've seen the movies. You know the songs. I am so used to the idea that my body was made for consumption that sometimes I forget it is mine.

Ignoring the way you look becomes a political act when you've been fetishized your entire life. It's a statement to be silent about your appearance when the world has been screaming about your hair, your face, your eyebrows, your feet, your armpits, your ass, your chest, your weight, your proportions, your striations, your various cuts of meat. And then, if you do speak—how brave!

There is an imagined afterlife or perfect alternate universe or some elevated state of existence where there is no such thing as being hot. Where we are all just beams of light, flitting around and illuminating whatever is in our noncorporeal path. In this universe, we mean it when we say we're wearing makeup just for ourselves because beams of light don't have cheekbones or pouty lips. If I were a beam of light, I hope that I would no longer care about my blackheads or my coffee-stained teeth. I hope I would relish in the freedom of not having this human body.

Is there anything so embarrassing as having a human body? My dog has no opinion on the eye boogers that get caught in the overgrown fur on her face, or the fact that I see them on her and could judge her for them. Birds don't know what a waistline even is. I'm body negative in that I believe no one should have a body. We should all be brains in jars that can mimic the feeling of playing tennis or smelling cinnamon or eating a lemon or hearing the ping of a text from your crush or getting canceled on Twitter by merely thinking about it.

This is all made more complicated by the fact that *looking* nice and *acting* nice have a complicated relationship. One that is both symbiotic and parasitic. First, we have the cultural notion that an abundance of one makes up for a lack of the other. Is the friend you're trying to set me up with hot? Uh, not in the conventional sense . . . but *she's nice though.* Is Henry Golding chill in real life? I don't know, but he's so hot I'd let him run me over with a car. Then, we have the unavoidable truth that nothing is so loathsome as a hot person who has the audacity to also be nice. Like, no, don't you get it? You won! You're hot! You get to live life with your face and body, and the consolation prize to the rest of us is that we get to whisper about how you were maybe kind of a bitch to us one time five years ago. Being hot and nice is comparable to connecting two positive poles on a magnet. It's as close to god tier as we mere mortals can get.

I know I don't have a realistic sense of how I look to other people. I have wondered if half my face looks more Asian than the other and which of those halves is my "good side." I've wondered whether the way I look will always come with an addendum about my race. I am pretty for a half-Asian girl. I shouldn't put my hair in a tight bun because it makes my eyes look . . . well, *you know*. I am exotic. I am foreign. I am front and center of your corporate photo shoot because, at best, I am ambiguous. Sometimes I look in the mirror and wonder if I've always been this ugly. Sometimes I think that Bella Hadid might look at me like her equal if I wore the right outfit.

I don't think being or feeling hot should be a goal. I don't wish to be told "Everyone is beautiful" by bottles of soap or Instagram models sponsored by ass bleach. I don't want to clap for conventionally hot people posting unfiltered photos or clothing companies who equate "body diversity" to the inclusion of conventionally hot people who happen to have flatter chests or are a little bit short.

I want to separate myself not just from the negative stories about body image but all stories that say happiness is dependent on finding yourself attractive. That loving yourself is contingent on assigning any value to how you look. I want to feel confident without having to ask anyone, myself included, whether I look okay. I also still want to watch every single celebrity's skin care routine. Baby steps.

In the rare moments I do feel hot, I'm usually by myself, and I feel like I need to say it out loud to acknowledge that, yes, there was a moment where I felt grateful to exist in this body.

It's a quiet kind of comfort to like yourself when you're alone.

WOMEN FOR DECORATION

Inspired by "The Semplica Girl Diaries,"*
by George Saunders

It looks like rain today. What will happen if it rains? Will someone bring us umbrellas? Will the van come early? We'd probably have to share an umbrella, if they brought one at all. The company said it doesn't rain much in this area, but how often is "much"? We've been lucky so far, I mean, as far as the weather goes. It's been warm and sunny. If I close my eyes, maybe I can be at the ocean.

I'm not sure who I'm thinking these thoughts for. I don't think this is praying—no, because I stopped doing that after the first week here. Praying felt like asking, and I'm tired of hoping for answers or wondering if no answer is actually an answer. Also, I don't think God is listening. You aren't, God, right? I guess I'm just thinking this for myself. Or my future self. Or maybe for someone else entirely who, years and years from now, has the technology to suck all my past thoughts from my brain. To put them in a book or a museum, to use

---

* I know, I'm surprised I wrote a short story too. Just go with it. Also, you don't have to read the original story to understand this one, but I highly recommend you do. If only so you can brag that you read not one but two short stories.

for research or maybe just for fun. If that's the case, I should probably introduce myself. It's only polite.

I am called a Semplica Girl. I am named for a doctor (Dr. Semplica) who figured out how to put a microfiber—it's like a thin string that's softer than wire but sturdier than thread. Anyway, years and years ago, he figured out how to string a microfiber through a person's head in a safe way, in a way that's not supposed to hurt. So, the fiber goes in one side of my temple, through my head, out the other side, and then goes into the next girl and the next. However many are ordered. Then, we're strung a few feet off the ground, each side of the microfiber attached to a tall, pretty pole in rich people's yards all around the world. Like a fancy clothesline but we're the clothes.

Speaking—thinking?—of clothes, I finally got a new frock. It looks exactly the same as the other one: white, down to my knees, flowy, and a little itchy. Still, it's nice to have something new. Who do you think makes our frocks? (If you're God or a time traveler, I'm waiting here a little for you to answer . . . okay, I'll keep going.) Maybe it's not a "who" that makes the frocks at all. I guess it had to start with someone, somewhere, carefully stitching the hem, tugging and smoothing until the fabric laid exactly how they wanted. And then they showed the frock to someone else and that person said, "What about white?" But the first person asked, "Wouldn't that get dirty?" And a third person chimed in and said, "How could they get dirty in midair?" And then, they all agreed that white was best and sent the design to a factory, and now a machine makes all our frocks. Machines can do a lot of things: make clothes, grind coffee, drive cars, trick grandparents. But I'm pretty sure there will always be Semplica Girls.

This is probably boring, sorry. It's not a very exciting job. A lot of quiet and hanging out (ha ha). A lot of time to think. The family has interesting jobs. The father does something important—the fathers always do. He wears ties and uses a briefcase, which I thought was just a thing on TV, but apparently they do it in real life too. I guess I don't really know what his job is, but he takes a lot of phone calls in the yard and he's usually talking about how "numbers are doing." He definitely has money—the families always do. Maybe he sells things? Or buys things? Tells people which things to sell and buy? Anyway, it's kind of a fun game to try to figure out his job—helps pass the time at least.

The mother is popular on the internet. I didn't have to guess, she showed us the day we arrived. Held her phone up and scrolled with her finger. (It didn't seem like we were allowed to touch.) Her phone is filled with pictures of her in the mirror, in the kitchen, in the garden—the flowers changing to match her. She's very beautiful. Everything about her is clean and bright and soft all at the same time. Once, I asked if she was famous and she laughed and said no, people just like seeing a "slice of my life." She makes everything look like a well-portioned pie, each piece precise and gorgeous, delicious and light. She used to show us the numbers—views, likes, followers—going up in real time on her page, but then the numbers got too big. I also asked if she was a model and she laughed even harder. She said she's "too real" to be a model.

She doesn't talk to us as much as she used to. That's fine. She used to say "How are you?" and then pull back a little like it was a habit she was trying to break. We'd say we're good and that the sun was nice or the breeze was nice and she'd agree. Sometimes she'd ask if she could get us anything even though she knows that's not allowed. Once, the company van came while she was handing us lemonade. (The van comes three times a day—6:00 a.m., 1:00 p.m., and 8:00 p.m. They take us down, give us food, let us freshen up a bit.) The person from the company got mad at us because he thought we'd asked for the lemonade, and the mother said, "No, no I offered! It's okay!" Then he thought she was trying to cover for us so he said she could tell him if we made her feel bad or about any "suspicious behavior." But she said, "No, no! It's okay! I wanted them to feel comfortable, but I understand if it's against your protocol." He let us finish the lemonade, probably because she gave him a glass too. She brought us things a couple times after that—water, cookies, sunscreen on an extrahot day—but eventually she stopped. It's fine, though, because imagine being up here and having to pee. Or worse. The mother will still smile if we're looking at each other at the same time. Then I'll smile too, which makes her smile a little bigger.

Oh, I should tell you about Jacinta. She is the other Semplica Girl here. She's very pretty. It's good I can't really turn my head because I'd probably stare at her too much. Like how you'll see a bird and think, *Huh, I didn't know birds could be that blue in real life.* Jacinta is pretty in a way that I didn't know people could be pretty in real life.

I'm not jealous. At least, I don't think I am because I don't think I'm ugly. I mean, I know I'm not because Semplica Girls can't be. It's not an official requirement, like being between eighteen and twenty-four or good customer service. But everyone knows you have to be pretty to be an SG. (I don't feel like thinking out the whole thing anymore. Just know when I think "SG" I mean Semplica Girl.) Back home, it was kind of a compliment. "You'd make so much money if you were an SG." "Are you an SG? Because I would let you hang around any day." Stuff like that. When we first started, I asked Jacinta if people told her those things growing up, but she said her mouth got her in too much trouble for that.

Jacinta used to tell me stories at night, about boys she'd met or SGs who made enough money to buy three houses. I think she was lying, but it was still fun. Jacinta could make the most boring things fun. We don't really talk anymore, even at night when the family's asleep and the company's done with their nightly rounds. It's boring, but it makes Jacinta feel safe.

I don't think Jacinta would mind me telling you this. Maybe just keep it between us though? Back when we were still new—not brand-new but the mother still asked how we were doing every day—the family threw a party. The daughter—oh, they have a daughter. And a son. I'll tell you—or "think" you? I'm still getting used to this. I'll think more about him later. Anyway, the daughter was turning one and the mother and father had a big party. There were two different cakes, a big balloon display that said ONE, and they even put a flower in my and Jacinta's hair so we'd match the rest of the decorations. The mother was worried because she didn't have orchids for us—they'd used the extras on the gift table. Jacinta suggested using flowers from the garden that were a similar color, and the mother got kind of mad and said that everyone would be able to tell the difference but she grabbed the flowers anyway. When guests started showing up, a couple said they liked the "attention to detail" and pointed to our hair. The mother said "thank you," and Jacinta whispered "you're welcome" to me, but I think the mother might have heard.

The guests were mostly adults, friends of the mother and father, but I recognized a couple of the children. One who I think is a neighbor, another who dressed as a Semplica Girl for Halloween. (The mother took a picture of the girl with me and Jacinta.) Some children, mostly little girls, look at us the same way you'd look at a puppy missing a part. Is that too sad? Sorry, if it is. You don't need to feel sad about it. I chose to be here, I was lucky enough to be chosen. When I'm done, I'll make money, my family will get money. The hardest part is missing my family, but think about it this way: it's kind of like I'm getting paid to miss my family. I feel like you're probably still sad. Anyway, I don't know if I ever saw the daughter at the party. I probably did but just don't remember. I did see the son though.

The son and another young boy, both even younger than my brothers, kept sneaking over by us all night. At first they tried to jump out and scare us, but Jacinta and I are very hard to startle. They never got close enough to touch us or anything. The company says the families are not supposed to touch us, but sometimes they do, like when you brush against a statue in a museum without looking at it. That way if anyone notices, you can say, *Oops, sorry, just an accident.* The boys kept their distance for the most part. But when they got bored of trying to scare us, they joked about what would happen if they stood right underneath us, about what they would see. "I bet Susanna's is smooth like a doll," the other boy laughed. Susanna is the name the company gave Jacinta—we all have company names, ones that are "less of a mouthful" and easier for the families to say, should they ever need to. Mine is Lisa. "Ha ha ha." The son laughed. "And I bet Lisa's got a big bush!" "Ew!" Then, Jacinta looked down at them and said, "Teeth."

BOYS: What?
JACINTA: There are teeth under there.
BOYS: Yeah, right. You're lying.

Then, Jacinta did a *chomp-chomp* thing with her teeth and the boys ran away. We laughed until it hurt, which was a mistake because we got in trouble. We both did but Jacinta got it worse. It's not my place to say what happened, but Jacinta doesn't talk or laugh or smile much anymore. Not unless she has to.

The day after the party, when the van came, I heard someone from the company say they could get a replacement for Jacinta, but the mother said something about it being too expensive. (I don't feel expensive. But if Jacinta and I are "expensive," what are big balloon displays for babies or gardens that change twice a week?) The father got a little red when she said the thing about us being "expensive"— he was mad or embarrassed, it's hard to tell which. "It's not about *money*," he said, a thing people with a lot of money like to say. It's funny what they'll say in front of us because they think we don't understand. That's probably why they said so much about Jacinta right in front of her. We actually have to speak pretty fluently to even be eligible for this region. The company said they could still just let her go, but the father insisted she stay. "Having just one Semplica Girl is more embarrassing than having none, ha ha ha." So, it's still the two of us. It's nice not to be alone, but it feels wrong to be glad for company. Especially after what happened to Jacinta.

The clouds are moving quickly today. Does that mean it's more likely to rain? Why am I thinking so much about rain? I never think about rain. I've thought about nearly everything a person can think about since I got here: my mama, my brothers, my school friends, my best friend and what she's doing right now, my birthday, the new year, that orange cake Mama made for my brother's birthday, the pregnant dog I passed every day on the way to school, whether she had her puppies, how many puppies she had, how many were girls, what their names would be, whether dogs name their puppies, what I'd name a puppy, what I'd name a daughter, whether she'd look like me, whether she'd notice the small scars on my temple, whether everyone will notice, whether I remember how my favorite foods taste. Jacinta told me I should think less and just count or something. I tried that once but lost track after 23,751.

Actually, I stopped because that was the day the mother came to talk to us about the party. I think a few weeks had already passed, but sometimes a day and a month feel the same up here. She said she wanted to apologize for what happened at the party and that she'd been thinking about it a lot and how it was probably just a "cultural difference" and she still wanted us to feel comfortable and that she was thinking about taking Mandarin. We said thank you and that we don't know Mandarin either. When she left she said "I'm sorry" again, but this time in a singsongy way, like how she kind of sings when she says "you're welcome."

You're WEL-come, I'm SO-rry, You're WEL-come, I'm SO-rry. She says the two the same way.

It's true that it doesn't hurt. Sometimes the microfiber itches a little, but it doesn't hurt. We were asleep for the whole procedure. When I woke up, I was already in my frock. The stringing up part is annoying but that also doesn't hurt. At first I thought they'd need us to be asleep during that, too, mostly because I didn't know how much we were allowed to see. But we need to hold ourselves still while they attach and remove the strings from the poles—so we're centered, spaced out evenly, etc.—and that's easier to do when we're awake.

Falling asleep here was hard at first, mostly because I had to get used to the quiet. But the company gives us something with our 8:00 p.m. food that makes it easier to sleep. I've actually never gotten more sleep, better sleep, in my life than I have here. I get tired around sundown and wake up with the sun, like a bird or a flower. You know some flowers sleep? Or I guess "sleep." (If I think of a word in air quotes, do you know there's air quotes? Sorry if that's obvious, I just want to make sure.) So, some flowers curl their petals inward at night, like they're tucking themselves in. It's to protect against the cool weather or predators—that's what scientists think. They don't really know for sure. At least, I'm pretty sure they don't know for sure.

I think it's cute. Flowers get all cozy when it's dark and stretch out in the morning. I also think it's cute that flowers turn toward the sun. I know they do it because they have to for energy and I know *they* don't know they're doing it, but *I* know they're doing it. It's like we have the same routine, like they're getting ready for work when we are. Their job is to sit in the sun and grow. Maybe the sun is their boss?

Some people think the family is our boss but they're not. The company is our boss—they're the ones who tell us what to do, what not to do, when to use the bathroom and change our frocks. The family pays for us, but the company makes the rules about how long we stay here and what we get paid. The family is like our . . . customer? The company just calls them our families so I guess "families" is the technical term. But the family is no more our bosses than they are the boss of the flowers, you know?

I don't like to think about this a lot but I heard a rumor that sometimes Semplica Girls are cut down. Some people say "freed" or "saved" or "let go." Jacinta said she heard about groups, kind of like charity groups, that go around and cut down SGs. But then what? Jacinta said she didn't know and I don't think she really cared. Jacinta talked a lot about how we could get down. Make our fingernails so sharp they cut the microfiber (impossible). Kick the person from the company in the crotch during the night round (I have bad aim). Convince the mother. That one didn't make any sense to me, but Jacinta said she's heard that sometimes it's the mother who cuts the SGs down. Or a daughter. For one, the mother doesn't listen to us. And two, she'd probably get in trouble and nobody wants that.

Like I told Jacinta, it's all going to pay off if we just do our best job. The company says we'll make enough money to do anything we want after. Anything. I don't know many former SGs but the ones I do know still send home money. It's easy to imagine an after, where I bring home a bunch of money. Where my mama and brothers have a bigger house and I have a room to myself. Or maybe I have a house of my own, two houses! We have huge dinners like we're having a party but it's just us. Every meal is my favorite meal. I get angry when I burn my mouth on something hot—I get to eat something hot! I wear long, soft frocks decorated with lots of jewels. It's so heavy I have people who help me carry it when I walk to dinner. Maybe I have a yard, a garden. Maybe I match my flowers, have SGs of my own. Sneak them lemonade and cookies. Throw parties where there are too many orchids to count. See? It's so easy but I try not to think too much about after. It feels like asking, too.

Oh, it's starting to rain. I hope we get an umbrella.

PART 3

Here to Make Friends

IT GIRL

My fascination with fame started as soon as I realized that real, human children were on TV and that I, too, was a real, human child. I worshipped at the altar of Mary-Kate and Ashley. I pretended to be cast member on the PBS show *Zoom*, explaining how to make stained glass for kids to an imagined camera. *All right, guys, now cut out a shape in the middle of a piece of printer paper, put Scotch tape over the hole, color on the tape using washable markers that'll get all over your fingers, lie to your parents when they ask who used all the paper and tape, and voilà! Stained glass!* When I'd hear a radio commercial for a mall event where scouts would be looking for new talent to cast on Disney Channel and Nickelodeon, I'd start thinking about the outfit I'd wear during my eventual debut red-carpet event. So, in second grade, when a magician came to my elementary school, he unknowingly brought with him the chance for me to publicly display my love of the limelight for the first time.

I don't remember why the magician was there. Maybe that qualified as our science lesson for the day. I do remember sitting in a makeshift row on the cafeteria floor, toward the front of a sea of seated students. For his next trick, the magician said he needed an assistant. I stared directly at him with glassy seven-year-old eyes. He searched the crowd briefly before looking back at me and asking, "Do you want to come up here and help?" It was equal parts an invitation and an acknowledgment that I'd been making unblinking eye contact with him for what felt like two solid minutes.

This was my moment or, rather, my premoment moment. First, I would have the entire school's eyes on me, and soon, the whole world would know my undeniable star quality. The mental leap from "Elementary School Magician's Assistant" to "Disney Channel It Girl" is difficult to make, but I'd taken gymnastics for, like, a year. This was my chance to be discovered by the talent scouts most certainly hidden among my peers, sitting cross-legged on a sticky school floor in Glendale, Wisconsin. As I stood up, I wondered if I should introduce myself as "Mia" or go by my full name, "Amelia," which would perhaps work better when I transitioned from child star to serious adult actor. I walked to the front, careful not to step on the hands of my classmates. I couldn't begin my career by literally stepping on the little people. Once at the front, I turned to face the audience, feeling a rush of excitement I'd never experienced before.

Just kidding! I didn't feel excited because I never made it to the front because I never even stood up. When the magician asked if I wanted to be his assistant, I responded by immediately bursting into quiet tears and shaking my head no. After all the time I had spent dreaming about being seen, adored, admired, and beloved by so many people, starring in imagined plays and shows and cereal commercials, a tiny chance had presented itself to me and I was too scared to even respond out loud. "That's fine," the magician reassured before calling up a nonsobbing student.

I wanted to perform almost as badly as I wanted absolutely no one to look at me. I desperately sought the attention of others while also wanting to remain completely invisible, all the time, forever. I wanted what Banksy had. In truth, I think I've always been much more in love with the idea of attention than the actual attention itself.

When performers talk about how they knew they wanted to perform, they use phrases like "just came naturally" and "loved being the center of attention." They almost always include a story about growing up putting on shows for their family and basking in the sound of their applause. As a kid, I did have an obnoxious habit of putting on living room shows for my family, making my siblings perform original musical adaptations of "Three Billy Goats Gruff" or forcing my grandma to clap as I tried to sing the national anthem, restarting no fewer than seven times. I did not, however, have what you would call a calming stage presence. I couldn't remember lines I'd written for myself, much less memorize lines someone else had written.

This dream of being famous continued too long for it to be cute. It extended well into middle and high school, where I would often procrastinate writing essays under the delusion that maybe I'd become a celebrity overnight for no reason. I'd imagine being called out of class like, "Ms. Mercado, we have Jonathan Taylor Thomas on the phone and your limo is here." In seventh grade, I competed in the National American Miss Preteen Wisconsin pageant, leaving with a participation trophy and the newfound knowledge of how to walk in heels while adults rate you out of ten. I made my mom drive me to a dozen different casting calls for modeling gigs and voice-over auditions throughout high school into my freshman year of college. I never booked a thing, not even for Whiny Kid Begging for KFC or Sad Teen Who Made a Bad Choice.

I continued to ignore the mounting evidence that maybe I wasn't destined for stardom. In school productions, I played iconic roles like Person at the Ball in *Cinderella*, Saltshaker in *Beauty and the Beast*, and Crow #2 in *The Wizard of Oz*. The only lead role I was ever cast in involved me being mostly silent. I played the Ghost of Christmas Future in *A Christmas Carol*, a role that had a total of three lines, but at least I was the literal embodiment of death. Once, a director told me I was perfect for a role called "The Mute."

I couldn't tell you why I wanted to be famous. Probably for the same reason anyone else wants fame: Is there anything so delicious as the idea of being widely beloved? My fantasies never involved dream roles, duets with pop icons, or really doing anything at all. To me, fame was a montage of glamorous adoration. It was walking down a red carpet in an outfit that would slaughter all my exes. It was the performative shock of winning an award, charmingly stumbling through a list of thank-yous I'd been practicing since I could write my own name. It was interviews where they'd ask about my morning routine, my favorite snacks, who my inspirations were, how I managed to stay so humble. It was blooper reels where I'm making a silly face to the camera—I'd be such a goofball on set! It was autographs, photo shoots, and paparazzi pictures emblazoned with the *Us Weekly* logo. I wanted the kind of fame that came when you got discovered in a mall. Pre-Instagram, Hilary Duff–era, nostalgia-steeped fame.

One of the last auditions I ever went on was undoubtedly the most humiliating. It was for a traveling teen show choir and that's not even the reason why it was humiliating. I had to prepare a song and went with the very bold choice of "Don't Rain on My Parade" from *Funny Girl*. I'd never had a solo in my suburban high school choir and some misguided part of my brain thought, *I bet I could do Barbra Streisand*. At the audition, I reminded myself to breathe from my diaphragm, I gave the most midwestern delivery of the line "Life's candy and the sun's a ball of butter," and then I forgot the rest of the words. I stopped and looked at the accompanist, who took a measure to realize the pause wasn't me taking creative liberties with the song. The person I was auditioning for raised his eyebrows before asking if I wanted to start again and if I'm always this embarrassing. (He didn't say the last part out loud, but he might as well have.) I've blocked the rest of the singing audition from my brain.

Then, I had to do a dance audition. The other kids in leotards and character shoes were stretching so I mimicked them, hoping that when I bent forward, my Target leggings didn't show the entirety of my ass. It was a group dance audition, so I gathered with my other show choir hopefuls and tried to recall anything from the ballet class I took when I was five. We were told to follow along with the two instructors at the front of the class, like Simon Says with pas de bourrées.

When measured against the general population, I am a perfectly fine dancer. I can pick up simple choreography. I clap on the twos and the fours. I know the limits of my body and can do the Cupid Shuffle without embarrassing myself. However, during this dance audition, I completely beefed it. My brain and my body had never and will never be as disconnected as they were for those ten minutes. Someone had put my controls upside down and in reverse, and I looked like I was learning in real time what appendages were and that I had them. Then, one of the instructors said, "Okay, for the last few measures, just freestyle!" I would've rather bent over and shown my whole ass. While one girl with KARA written in rhinestones on her top did gorgeous leaps and another kid did some mediocre break dancing, I resorted to step-and-claps like someone who'd just stumbled upon a flash mob. I did not receive a callback.

I only ever told a small handful of people about these auditions, mostly so I would only have to tell a small handful of people that, no, I would not be Daughter #2 in an upcoming Wisconsin Department of Transportation radio spot. My quiet attempts at child stardom were both the antithesis and the definition of who I was.

I wanted fame without the possibility of public failure. I wanted to keep the dream alive and knew that keeping it in a state of limbo, where I didn't hear yes or no, was the only way to assure it'd never die. This secret pursuit of fame eventually fizzled out around the time I needed to declare a major in college.

I've spent so much of my life afraid of embarrassing myself that I've often stopped short altogether. I've spent an equal amount of time imagining the complete opposite, picturing a life where putting myself out there is only met with thunderous applause and record deals. In the past, when I've been handed small opportunities to be seen, I've pushed the hand away. I froze when asked to be the magician's assistant. I pulled out of the play when I was cast as "The Mute." Rather than be a silent side character, I chose not to be seen at all. A bold choice for someone convinced they were an undiscovered triple threat.

I can't imagine the kind of terror I would have caused had Instagram influencers and YouTubers been a formative part of my childhood. I don't know who I would have grown up to be had fame seemed that accessible, had I been able to potentially access a worldwide audience without leaving my bedroom. I looked at archetypal child stars like Mary-Kate and Ashley, and thought, *I could do that.* Think of the kind of damage I could have done had I seen people getting national attention for biting their sibling's finger or making salad in a pretty way.

There is no record of my failed attempts at fame. As far as I know, no one was secretly recording my show choir audition or live-tweeting the time I performed an acoustic song I'd written for a creative writing class. I'm not sure if the idea of going viral in a bad way would have quelched my desire for fame or simply stoked it. I was able to delete my bad, embarrassing high school blog before anyone would have googled my name. I know, because I've googled my name more than anyone, and any remnants of that bad, bad blog have never surfaced.

Now, I'm far more afraid of being too seen than being ignored. The internet is too big, anonymity can make people too mean, and I am too sensitive to want to be anything more than a recognizable byline. The teeny, tiny taste of online attention I've gotten from writing has been more good than bad, but guess which DMs and emails I remember the most? Guess which tweets I've had to block because Riley said I was "being obsessive" and "focusing on one person's mean comment" and that "No, I don't agree with the anonymous Twitter user that said the gap between your teeth is bigger than your cleavage. Please put your phone down and go to bed!"

I'm still grappling with the knowledge that attention and admiration are not one and the same, that part of my job and part of being alive today means that I will have an audience whether I want it or not. But I'm starting to realize that, maybe, it's okay if the seating is limited.

CAN I SIT HERE?

I wish I could retain information about actual politics as much as I can lunchroom politics. I can break down the hierarchy of who holds the most power in the *Gossip Girl* reboot, complete with annotations about which episodes proved to be pivotal turning points for which characters. But I sometimes forget that Ben Franklin wasn't a US president.

Though I've been out of high school longer than some high schoolers have been alive, the "Oh god, where am I gonna sit?" feeling definitive of school lunchrooms still lingers. It comes up when I arrive at a party alone where I only know one person and that person is the host. If the words *network* or *reunion* or *let's go around and introduce ourselves* are involved, I'll get anxiety-induced bubble gut thinking about who I'll seat myself next to before inevitably shitting my pants.

Now, at this proverbial lunchroom of Pop Culture High, here I stand, holding my lunch tray, as an entire adult in her thirties, asking famous young people the hypothetical question that my younger self desperately wanted answered: Can I sit with you?

LIZZIE MCGUIRE, GORDO, AND MIRANDA

Growing up, there were few TV characters I saw myself in as much as Lizzie McGuire. Played by Miss 2000s herself, Hilary Duff,

Lizzie was a hyperaccessible "every girl." She was often quiet and usually nice. Though she wasn't one of the cool kids, she had a solid group of friends: Gordo, a guy who pined for Lizzie from a-close and was the charmingly nervous embodiment of my imagined perfect boyfriend; and Miranda, played by the one-named Lalaine, who I have committed to memory because she, like me, is Filipina. Lizzie had unrequited crushes and reeked of teenage awkwardness. She was trying to figure out her own identity while still desperately seeking popularity. She felt familiar and extremely regular, something that, when I was younger, resonated in a way that idealized characters never did. Stars—they're just like me, specifically.

She was, of course, not regular at all. There's an episode where Lizzie *Freaky Fridays* with her younger brother, and they have to navigate going to school as each other. This leads to one of my favorite TV and movie tropes: an actor pretending to be someone pretending to be someone else, like a Russian nesting doll of acting. Later in the series, she kisses the titular Aaron Carter of "Aaron's Party (Come Get It)." Carter had a cameo as himself in an episode a couple years before he and Duff dated in real life. The two eventually broke up after Carter allegedly cheated on Duff with Lindsay Lohan—life imitating fan fiction. Lizzie even briefly switched lives with an Italian pop star named Isabella in *The Lizzie McGuire Movie*. In no universe was I anything like Lizzie McGuire.

Also, Lizzie's family often seemed like they were on a completely different show than her. Once, her younger brother, Matt, had a feud with a chimpanzee named Fredo. In another episode, Matt showcases his family's house as a "Dust Museum." In another episode still, Fredo the chimp does Matt's homework for him and gets a better grade. The show was nominated for an Emmy twice.

Regardless, I think Lizzie would've let me sit at her lunch table. She was nothing if not friendly and seemed approachable even to me, someone afraid of interrupting my Google Home. If anything, I could just swap places with Miranda and hope Lizzie didn't notice.

REGINA GEORGE, GRETCHEN WIENERS, KAREN SMITH

Of the three of these *Mean Girls*, I'd obviously be least afraid to approach Karen. I'd have an in because I'd let her cheat off me in social studies. She'd agree to let me sit next to her while she copied my notes during lunch, and I'd use this as a chance to say something disarming to Gretchen, like someone *should* just totally stab Caesar. Because she wouldn't see me as any type of threat, Gretchen would engage in conversation, and I would offer zero opinions and agree with everything she said. Regina wouldn't register me as human, but I'd still mimic the way she shook her salad in its plastic container to disperse the dressing as a sign of respect. Throughout the entirety of high school, Regina would never talk to me. But, years later, she would message me, out of the blue, to catch up and see if I'm interested in a supereasy way to make money from home.

CADY HERON, DAMIAN LEIGH, AND JANIS IAN

I also would not be cool enough to sit with Damian and Janis. Cady, maybe. But in *Mean Girls: I'm in This One Now*, Cady only lets me sit with her until everyone realizes how hot she is. Then she no longer requires a lunch table and is bestowed with a throne. Damian and Janis, however? There isn't even an imagined version where I have a wide enough breadth of pop culture knowledge and self-assurance where they'd tolerate my nervous little ass. I'd probably go eat lunch in Tina Fey's classroom.

THE CAST OF *THE O.C.*

Though I worshipped at the altar of L.C. on *The Hills*, drooled over Stephen on *Laguna Beach*, and still check in on Heidi and Spencer

"Speidi" Pratt, I never actually watched *The O.C.*, its fictional forefather, until recently. If you ever require entertainment that will make you say, "Huh, these hot people sure dress stupid," *The O.C.* is what you seek. It's peak 2005 opulence, which is to say, "ugly as hell." The clothes they brag about, the houses where they aspire to live, the amount of Mischa Barton's hip bones you see throughout the series could be described as campy were the show to take itself just a little bit less seriously.

The only person who I'd want to sit with at lunch—I've only watched the first season, so keep that in mind—is nerd loser Seth Cohen, played by Adam Brody. Were we to have gone to the same high school, I would have lost my goddamn mind for Seth Cohen. While Seth would obsess over Summer, the archetypal cool girl played by Rachel Bilson, I would obsess over Seth. He would probably mistake me for his maid's daughter.

THE GIRLS OF *HIGH SCHOOL MUSICAL*

The cultural reset that is *High School Musical* came out my sophomore year of high school. If you don't think I memorized the entirety of its soundtrack and learned the final dance number in my parents' living room, then we're clearly not all in this together. Did I long to be a Gabriella, the smart (how brave!) ingenue played by Vanessa Hudgens? Of course. It didn't help that Hudgens is half-Filipina, a piece of information I clearly cannot be trusted with lest it lead me to delusions like, "I could be Hilary Duff's best friend." I could have been a Taylor, Gabriella's also-smart friend played by Monique Coleman. She dates basketball player Chad, played by Corbin Bleu, and I am of the firm belief that he, not Troy Bolton, was the hottest guy on the team. (My type is either "dork loser who ignores me" or "boring jock who ignores me with muscles.") However, Taylor was more confident at fifteen than I am at double her age. So, were I to have gone to East High, I would not have been friends nor sat with either Gabriella or Taylor.

Surprisingly, I wouldn't have been afraid to ask if I could sit with Sharpay, the self-described school queen bee played by Ashley Tisdale. Sharpay was a theater kid. She probably did extracurricular singing groups, and we would have been in the chamber choir together. During the holidays, when we sang around the town in Dickensian Christmas outfits,* complete with hoopskirts and bonnets, she would have called dibs on the least ugly ensemble. We would have sat in the choir room with the rest of the kids whose personality was "Do you want to hear me sing?" drinking Snapple and talking shit on the cast list.

MARY-KATE AND ASHLEY OLSEN

I shouldn't admit the degree to which I was obsessed with Mary-Kate and Ashley growing up. I loved their feature-length films like *Passport to Paris*, *Winning London*, *When in Rome*, and *The Challenge*, which took place in Mexico. More movies should decide plotlines based on where the stars want to go on vacation. I longed to be on the guest list of one of the parties, sleepovers, or school dances the twins attended in *You're Invited to Mary-Kate and Ashley's*, the straight-to-video series that's also responsible for my personal national anthem, "Gimme Pizza." I still know all the words to the theme song of *The Adventures of Mary-Kate and Ashley*, a different straight-to-video series in which the twins solve mysteries like, "Could a ghost be haunting this abandoned mansion?" and "Hey, is that a dead body?" In the latter, the girls walk around SeaWorld with a basset hound, find a dead body in the woods, take money from buskers so they can go on a cruise, and find out that the dead body was actually just a mime

---

* Yes, this is an actual thing my high school did. It was very fun and, I gotta be honest, the costumes weirdly made me feel . . . kinda hot?

pretending to be a dead body. The Olsen twins absolutely deserve every penny they've earned.

I can't pinpoint what it was about Mary-Kate and Ashley I loved so much. Maybe it was the fact that these two young girls had taken over television, movies, Walmart's preteen clothing department, and the world before they could drive. Maybe it was my fascination at the idea of there being two of me. It was probably a combination of both sprinkled with my own desire to be a child star (not to be confused with being an actor).

Would Mary-Kate and Ashley have let me sit at their lunch table? I think so, if only as an extra in one of their movies.

MANNY FROM *DEGRASSI: THE NEXT GENERATION*

I attribute much of my teen horniness to *Degrassi*. It was the soapy high school drama I craved as a very boring high schooler. Something extremely traumatic happened quite literally every episode. This, if nothing else, gave me a morbid escape from my deeply regular teenage problems. There's Aubrey Graham, as in the rapper Drake, playing a character named Jimmy who is paralyzed after a school shooting. In one of the most gut-wrenching moments on all of television, a sweet little dweeb named J.T. is stabbed to death at a birthday party. (Why did I like this show??) *Degrassi* had people getting pregnant, self-harm, eating disorders, abuse—if it's something that would make my parents say, "Amelia Lourdes, what is this?" it was a plotline on *Degrassi*. There's also an episode where a character named Emma gets gonorrhea after performing oral sex. This terrified my younger sister, who believed oral sex was "just when you talk about it." She spent the next year thinking that you could get an STI from mentioning intercourse.

But my personal favorite story line of the entire series was the on-and-off, sometimes unrequited relationship between Craig and Manny. Craig was the brooding upperclassman who played music and had a complicated relationship with his dad. (It's like the show writers read my journal and created a hot bad boy just for me.) He was played by Jake Epstein, who I later saw in a production of *Spring Awakening*. In addition to meeting James Van Der Beek (more on that soon), my claim to fame is that I got to see Craig from *Degrassi*'s ass during that show. Manny starts as a sweet, naïve underclassman often obsessed with popularity and eventually becomes . . . well, a lot of different things. Manny is played by Cassie Steele, who is—say it with me—Filipina!

Of all the Mannys we see in *Degrassi*—Manny who is cute and shy, Manny who gets an abortion, Manny who stars in a musical by Jason Mewes aka Jay of *Jay and Silent Bob*—the very best Manny is Thong Manny. In a ploy to prove to the boys that she isn't just cute, Manny gives herself a horny makeover. In her words, "I wanna be hot! Not cute. Not adorable. HOT!" Reader, she makes herself look hot.

She enters the school wearing a newsboy cap—already a bold choice. Her lips? Glossed. Her cheeks? Rouged. Her shoulders? Exposed in an off-the-shoulder peasant top. She's also wearing a bra with straps that she keeps pushed off her shoulders because knowing that someone is wearing a bra? Peak sex appeal. However, the pièce de résistance of the outfit is on display courtesy of the lowest-rise jeans science could create: a bright blue thong with tiny rhinestone embellishments. Not only is her thong above her pants in the back, you can see it in the front, too. The audacity! The nerve! I know that I bought my first thong after watching that episode.

Would Manny have let me sit with her? Pre-thong, maybe. Post-thong, not a chance.

THE WOMEN NAMED IN "MAMBO NO. 5"

I would watch a feature-length film on the women Lou Bega name-drops in his 2000 banger "Mambo No. 5." There's Angela, Pamela,

Sandra, Rita, Monica, Erica, Tina, Mary, Jessica, and also the trumpet, which, though not a woman, is definitely a love interest. I want to know more about these ladies! Where did he meet them? Do they know one another? What are their thoughts on the order of their mention and the fact that Lou says some of their names in a verse along with the chorus? Did he make them sit and listen as he tried to play the trumpet? Did they have to be like, "Yeah, that's great, Lou, but can we get back to the line where you say, 'You can't run and you can't hide'? Is that a threat??" Has he even spoken to any of these women?

This is the lunch table where I'd long to be, with a dozen women all dishing dirt on the mustachioed Lou Bega and devising a scheme to inspire "Mambo No. 6."

HERE TO MAKE FRIENDS

I didn't let myself watch *The Bachelor* franchise until recently because I knew what it would do to me. I knew I'd get too invested in the mediocre white men trying to find love and/or the tiniest brunette with the highest butt. I knew I'd spend hours googling whether contestants have to bring their own gowns (they do), how many couples are still together (at the time I'm writing this, just eight of all the pairs put together over the past forty-four seasons), whether any Asian men had ever made it to the final four (LOL, JK, I didn't have to google this to know the answer is "literally only one"; there have been more white guys named Chris in the final four than Asian men). I knew I'd love it, I knew I'd hate it, and I knew I'd absolutely love hating it.

Unlike my husband, Riley, who has been known to be like, "You wanna watch this three-hour-long opus on the Mafia at nine in the morning?," my taste in movies and TV varies pretty drastically depending on my mood, the time of day, whether or not I've eaten, etc. On a mellow evening, I can get with an independent film that has more of a vibe than a plot. After spending hours scrolling through awful news, my brain goes, *Now would be a great time to watch a ten-part docuseries on a murderer nicknamed Big Yucky Rape Man.* I can get myself in the mood to fall in love with beautiful people falling in love so long as I'm emotionally prepared to spend the next hour thinking about all the things I would/wouldn't do if I was hot enough to get away with it. But no matter what, I will always, always watch something that I know is going to be shitty.

Perhaps part of it is just pure fascination with what networks are willing to air. I never cease to be amazed by the things that get made. So many shows sound like a network exec got very high during a pitch meeting and was like, "What if there was a cutthroat competition . . . but the prize . . . was love???"

Here are just a few examples:

Actual adults green-lit a show called *Kid Nation*, in which forty kids ages eight to fifteen spent forty days living unsupervised in a ghost town where they had to make their own food, care for themselves and each other, and start their own community / commune / *Lord of the Flies* adaptation. Clips still exist on YouTube if you really want to go down a child labor rabbit hole.

There were nearly two hundred episodes and two different revivals of *Fear Factor*, a show that gave $50,000 to people who could endure "challenges" like being electrocuted, being tear-gassed, and drinking "smoothies" made of blended-up rats.

There have been multiple seasons of *The Masked Singer*, a reality competition that essentially boils down to C-list celebrities doing karaoke in elaborate furry costumes while Jenny McCarthy asks Robin Thicke, "Oh my god, do you think that could be Beyoncé?!?"

Reality TV covers a vast range of content, from the soap opera-esque drama of *The Hills* or *Keeping Up with the Kardashians* to HGTV home makeover porn. But if there is one brand of reality TV that speaks to my nasty lil soul, it is reality competitions. Shows that assemble a cast of hot narcissists, hot aspiring Instagram influencers, and one or two kind-of-regular people who are, get this, also very hot in a house and just . . . see what happens. Shows with only half-thought-through challenges that production assistants are probably made to come up with after someone remembers, "Oh yeah, these people are supposed to be, like, competing or something." Shows where someone inevitably says those six little words producers and viewers love to hear: *I'm not here to make friends!*

Save for *The Great British Bake Off*—a baking competition that is essentially a visual Xanax—no reality series is safe from the contestant who asserts they aren't there for friendship. There are YouTube compilations from every kind of reality competition—*Survivor*, *Project Runway*, *Rock of Love*, even the Food Network's *Chopped*—where the producer-designated "villain" of the season declares that they are not, in fact, here to be buddy-buddy with the other contestants. This proclamation is sometimes said in a confessional interview, other times it's said directly to another contestant's face to really drive the "fuck you" home. It usually happens after a confrontation and is accompanied by phrases like "not afraid to say what's on my mind" and "I don't care if people don't think I'm nice."

"I'm not here to make friends" is an assertion that made more sense when reality television existed in something of a vacuum. You'd compete on a reality show, maybe take part in a spin-off show, and then go back to living whatever private life you led beforehand.

Reality TV and the postshow potential of its contestants has changed entirely since the early 2000s. Now when you sign up for a reality show, what you're actually hoping to land are those spin-offs, along with endorsement deals, book contracts, sponsored posts, paid content, and the chance to be named the "creative director" of some pseudohealth gummy that will bleach your asshole for you. Where once upon a time people were cast in reality TV "roles" and then released back into their regular existence, they now trade details of their personal lives for brand deals that will pay them way more than six weeks on *Bachelor in Paradise* ever would. We are in the middle *Animorph* stage of this transformation from reality star to social media celebrity where everything is blurry and comes with a promo code for 10 percent off nipple pasties.

There is no longer a need for me to scour the internet to find where *Love Island* contestants are now because my Instagram feeds it to me. I'm given updates on the siblings of former contestants of *The Circle*. I'm told when to congratulate reality TV couples that have gotten back together after breaking up after getting back together. Saying "I'm not here to make friends" made a lot more sense when you weren't, at least in some part, hoping to gain followers.

While I pretended not to care about *The Bachelor* for years, I wasted no time diving headfirst into the British dating show *Love Island* the second I found out about its existence. *Love Island* is a UK dating competition that puts singles together in a villa (British for "horny mansion") for a few weeks. They compete to find love and be part of the final couple that wins £50,000—a prize that seems like a pittance in comparison to the tens of thousands contestants stand to earn from a few sponsored Instagram posts after the show. Yes, I am Neo seeing all the workings of the Matrix but getting distracted by the secret agents' skin care routines.

There's an episode in HBO's *Euphoria* where Zendaya's character Rue is so depressed all she can do is lie in the dark and watch *Love Island*. It's a scene that's a little too familiar to me, listening to the narrator's opening "PREviously on *LOVE Island*" as I lie to myself about taking a shower after I finish this episode. Something about my broken brain loves seeing hot people from all over the UK say things like "He's prop-ah fit" and "She's 100 percent my type on pay-puh." I love that the UK equivalent of "I'm not here to make friends" is "I'm not afraid to step on people's toes." I love deluding myself into thinking I can do a believable Essex accent or that I could even point out Essex on a map. I love seeing hot people quickly fall in summer-camp love, the kind of love I remember feeling for any boy who'd look at me during the weeklong summer church camp I attended in high school. When you spend nearly all your waking hours around someone, some part of your brain unlocks or breaks down and you think, *Yeah, I could picture myself starting a life with Forest, a kid from Georgia I met two days ago and whose last name I do not know.*

"I bet we could win *Love Island*" is something Riley and I say to each other every time we start a new season of the show. We've watched all seven seasons currently available on Hulu, which works out to be about 350 forty-five-minute episodes. Combined, that'd almost be eleven full days of watching *Love Island* nonstop—no sleeping, no looking away to google a contestant's age, no looking at each other like, *Are we okay?* However, that total amount of time doesn't account for the fact that we've watched a couple seasons through twice.

To be clear, we definitely could not win *Love Island.* The two of us combined don't have nearly enough abs or swimsuits to make it past the initial casting. Even if we got to the villa, I would absolutely spend most days crying about how I have no idea how to get rid of my pube stubble. He'd be sent home after he tried to sneak a duffel bag of LEGO bricks on set to have something to do. Also, we're already married.

The *Love Island* application for the US spin-off* is much less intimidating than I would have expected. While it asks for handles

---

* Initially, the US version affirmed what Riley and I already suspected to be true: we mostly like *Love Island* because of the accents. We couldn't make it past episode one of the US's first season. But then the pandemic hit and the second season came out, and now I often wonder whether a guy named Carrington was a real contestant on the show or if he was just Andy Samberg doing an impression of an influencer.

for your Instagram, Twitter, Facebook, etc., it doesn't overtly ask how many followers you have. It doesn't ask for your height, weight, and whether or not you have kids, like the *Bachelor* application does. It has standard questions like "Are you genuinely looking for a relationship?" and "Tell us something surprising about your life that we would never know." I would pay upward of $500 to see the answers of people who actually got cast on the show. The application for this dating competition also asks "Are you single?" and the drop-down menu reads "YES" or "NO." (The *Bachelor* application doesn't include this question despite the fact that most every season, there's one contestant with a secret girlfriend back home.) I'm not sure whether to take this question as *Love Island*'s commitment to finding people who are "actually looking for love" or if they technically . . . allow people who aren't single. Do they see someone's current "in a relationship" status as evidence that they are ready to find love and not, oh I don't know, a red flag?

Because I cannot help but make everything about me, I've thought about how I'd act as a contestant on *Love Island* more than I should admit. I've wondered how I'd fare in challenges like "Shaken or Stirred,"* where contestants have to make cocktails by passing the individual ingredients mouth to mouth, or "Girl Power," a "superhero" challenge where the female contestants assert their heroic strength by trying to break a watermelon with their ass. Mostly, I wonder if I'd make any friends.

The roots of this curiosity go back to my first and most formative

---

* There have been versions of this game where contestants make everything from fruit smoothies to milkshakes to hamburgers, passing and receiving each ingredient with their mouths. The latter involved the contestants passing mouthfuls of ketchup and mustard to each other, like a section of Porn-Hub you accidentally stumbled into.

reality TV obsession: *America's Next Top Model.* The series debuted in 2003, the same year I turned thirteen. It was all long legs, dramatic makeovers, host Jay Manuel guiding the girls to find their light, judge J. Alexander walking better than the contestants ever could, supermodel Janice Dickinson's life-ruining criticism masquerading as maternal tough love, and women posing uncomfortably but in a hot way. It had "go-sees" (a challenge that manifested my exact brand of teen anxiety), in which contestants had to see as many prospective clients as possible on an impossibly tight schedule. It had Tyra Banks at peak Tyra Banks. It was destined to rule and ruin my adolescence.

The series is perhaps best known for its bits that seeped into the greater culture: the instant meme-ification of Tyra yelling "I was rooting for you" at contestant Tiffany Richardson in cycle four (the series inexplicably had cycles instead of seasons) and Banks's nonsense vocabulary dubbed by many as "Tyra-speak," which gave us phrases like *booch* and *tooch* (verb; to pop one's booty) and words like *smize* (verb; to smile with one's eyes). Fun fact: the word *smize* was coined in cycle thirteen, the same season that had a "biracial photo shoot," which involved headdresses, appropriative costuming, and skin-darkening makeup. Smize through the systemic oppression, girlies!

Cycle one of *ANTM* had an entire plotline around a contestant's virginity, a topic that, one would argue, should be completely irrelevant to your job. It has episodes with titles like "The Girl Who Everyone Thinks Is Killing Herself"—roughly forty-two minutes spent postulating about a contestant's eating disorder—and "The Girl Who Deals with a Pervert," in which eventual cycle one winner Adrianne Curry is groped by a complete stranger in Paris. Aside from the episode title and a thirty-second clip of the harassment taking place, the incident isn't addressed. The show was, in a word, bad.

Until recently, most of this escaped my memory entirely. What thirteen-year-old me fixated on was limited to glossy photos, make-over montages, and the impossible coolness of 2003 Tyra Banks. I remember panic-sweating as contestants got lost on the way to go-sees. I remember hearing women in low-rise jeans say they didn't come to make friends, they came to become America's Next Top Model (cue theme song).

Watching *ANTM* planted a seed in my head that, yeah, sure, I could be a model if I really wanted to. I could audition for the competition with a runway walk that showed potential. I could take direction from Tyra during photo shoots. I could sit in a makeup chair without fidgeting and pose in swimsuits during the winter without complaining. I could act like I'm there for the right reasons and pretend those reasons aren't "needing constant external validation." I could make enough friends to fit in in the house without inserting myself into drama. I could keep myself from being the Bitchy One, the Emotional One, the One Who Parties Too Much. I could hope to be the Crowd Favorite or the One Who Everyone Knows Is Going to Win, but I'd settle for the Nice One. I could be the Nice One. She's not really anyone's favorite, but she definitely isn't anyone's least favorite. She wouldn't get as much airtime, but at least you won't see her break down on-screen. She probably wouldn't be memorable or interesting or win, but she wouldn't lose any friends. At least people would still assume she's nice. Though I tried to germinate this seed by going to a small handful of casting calls in middle and high school, it never really sprouted, and thank god.

I don't know what reality show I'd be equipped for now. I'm too bad at directions and getting lost without crying for *The Amazing Race*. I'm too sensitive to criticism for *American Idol*. I'm too poor for *Real Housewives*. Too married for *Love Is Blind*. Too agnostic and IUD-ed up for *19 Kids and Counting*. I don't know if I'm living vicariously through these people whose lives I absolutely do not want or if I'm convincing myself I am somehow better or smarter or more good for merely observing these shows rather than trying to partake in them. I don't know why I continue watching things I hate, why maybe, deep down, I do love these shows but hate that I love them. I wish I didn't get tiny bursts of serotonin every time I angrily dissect the actions of a contestant I am convinced has agreed to play the role of the Bitch. I wish I didn't have the instinct to look up every single contestant on Instagram to see if TV them is the same as internet them and if either of those versions seem like who they actually are.

In my blurry mental montage of panels of judges, elimination ceremonies, and the chorus of "Can I steal you for a sec," the contestants I remember most vividly from every reality series are either the people I loved or the people I loved to hate. Maybe I'm not here for the right reasons. Maybe I'm not trying to make friends after all.

KILL THEM WITH KINDNESS AND OTHER IMAGINED CRIME PODCASTS

KILL THEM WITH KINDNESS: An investigation into the serial killer whose calling card was saying "sorry!" after she poisoned people.

DID YOU SEE THE ONE ABOUT THE CULT?: Two friends ask each other if they've watched the newest true crime docuseries on Netflix, usually involving pseudoreligious murder sex cults. The other says "Yes" and the first friend says, "Fucked up, right?" They go back and forth like this for fifty-five minutes.

GHOSTS?!: Talking to people who watch paranormal movies and say, "Okay, I don't, like, *believe* believe in ghosts, but I did use a Ouija board in seventh grade and it definitely worked."

HOW TO GET AWAY WITH MURDER: A series on how to turn your side hustle (murder) into a full-time gig (more murders) hosted by an entrepreneurial murderer who has tips on how aspiring serial killers can make their sprees more efficient.

ESPECIALLY HEINOUS: Dissecting the sexual tension between Detectives Elliot Stabler and Olivia Benson from *Law and Order: SVU*. Season two is told from the perspective of Christopher Meloni's ass.

PER MY LAST EMAIL: The story of a woman who used so many passive-aggressive exclamation points her computer exploded and destroyed a town.

OKAY, FINE, TED BUNDY: A podcast that aggregates every movie, show, and podcast retelling Ted Bundy's crimes and plays them all at once.

CHOPPED: A crime crossover series with the cooking competition *Chopped.* The mystery ingredient is always blood.

THE ADVENTURES OF MARY-KATE AND ASHLEY OLSEN: An audio reboot of the straight-to-video investigative series where the twins finally reveal how they killed off their triplet.

BAD BLOOD: Suppositions on, if Taylor Swift were to murder all her exes, where she would hide the bodies. Each episode description contains Easter eggs that always spell out *ocean.*

THE WELLBUTRIN CHRONICLES: Me talking about the first month I started the antidepressant Wellbutrin, and my only feelings were rage and more rage. Each episode would explore the things that made me angry (being hungry, I made a dumb typo, someone sent me an email with a very obnoxious subject line, the fact that I was angry over nothing thus making me angrier) and whether I was justified in that anger (I wasn't).

COLD CASES: A look at how anyone is able to survive a northern winter without committing multiple acts of violence.

CSI: MY BROWSER HISTORY: Connecting the dots between how I went from the Google search results of the *Mare of Easttown* cast to looking up "do dogs have accents."

CRIMINAL MINDS: A nostalgic podcast reminiscing on the times in college when I'd come home, take a three-hour nap, wake up to watch an episode of *Criminal Minds*, and pass out while looking at Google images of Matthew Gray Gubler.

LOVE ISLAND, AFTER DARK: This is less a podcast and more a YouTube compilation of all the night-vision shots from reality dating show *Love Island* where contestants are lying in bed, staring at the ceiling, eyes unblinking and aglow like horny demons.

JOHN DOE: My party trick is being able to identify which celebrities, when combined, look like another celebrity. This is also extended to the Pokémon evolutions for groups of two or more celebrities. For example, Rachel Brosnahan is a combination of Evan Rachel Wood and Brie Larson. Samara Weaving is the Charmander to Margot Robbie's Charmeleon, and Jaime King is their Charizard. On this podcast, listeners send in their own photos, and I tell them which combination of celebrities they look like, a game that is fun for me and me alone.

CAN I STEAL YOU FOR A SEC?: A series sussing out which *Bachelorette* contestants throughout the entire franchise were definitely serial killers. Every season has at least one. Sometimes it's obvious—once, there was a guy whose profession was "skin salesman."* Other times, it's implied based on a man's haircut and general vibe.

CHEATING DEATH: Recounting the moments in my life when I absolutely could have gotten murdered but did not. One episode explores the time I flew across the country to meet up with a guy I met on *checks notes* video chat website Omegle. Another is an exploration into the time my friend Sami and I hopped into the dilapidated van of a high school garage band we'd just watched play at the

---

* Yes, really. That's too terrible for even my wormy brain to have made up.

local American Legion building. Each episode ends with a message from our sponsors (my parents being like, "Amelia Lourdes, you did WHAT?!").

IN THE PODCAST, WITH THE BOOM MIC: A playthrough of the murder mystery board game Clue. Every episode devolves into a ranking of which characters sound the hottest and why number one is always Miss Scarlet. We also discuss how difficult it would actually be to kill someone with a candlestick.

FUCK, MARRY, KILL: In this narrative podcast, the hosts begin each episode with a round of the classic sleepover game in which you are given three people and decide who you'd have sex with, who you'd wed, and who you would murder. They then discuss the ramifications of these decisions. For example, if, in a breakfast-food-themed round, you say you would marry waffles over pancakes and French toast, does that mean you must eat waffles every single day? Which trio of Muppets leads to the most divisive choices? Do your husband, Crackle, and mistress, Pop, help you bury the body of Snap?

MOMMY'S STORIES: A multipart look at the people obsessed with true crime media. We'll talk to women who watch docuseries on dismembered corpses to fall asleep. We'll hear from people who wear shirts like MURDER IS MY LOVE LANGUAGE while pushing strollers. We'll take a closer look at people who hold their keys between their fingers while walking through a dark parking garage and, once safely inside their car, unpause their podcast about a serial rapist with an earlobe fetish. Finally, we'll answer the question everyone has been asking: "Y'all good?"

LIKE AND SUBSCRIBE

'm fairly certain the first video I watched on YouTube was "Dick in a Box," the *SNL* song by The Lonely Island featuring Justin Timberlake. The premise, if you somehow aren't familiar, is as follows: It's Christmas, and Andy Samberg and Justin Timberlake are going to gift their girlfriends their penises, which, as the title implies, are inside of a box. I'm equally certain that the person who showed me this video was my mom. I know, I am as surprised as you.

When I saw that video in 2006 or 2007, YouTube was still relatively new. I was mostly watching videos on websites like funnyjunk .com. I remember when it was possible, or at least *felt* possible, to have seen all the viral videos. The internet had an end, one that I'd often reach while I was supposed to be doing homework. The bar for virality was also much, much lower back then. If a video had a hundred thousand views, it was likely described as "going viral." Five hundred thousand views was full-on viral. A million views would propel you to YouTube infamy. Unlike today, where it's likely there are YouTube channels you've never heard of that somehow have millions of subscribers, when a video went viral, you saw it.

This, I would argue, was the birth of the influencer. (Or maybe the conception of the influencer? I don't know, social media and brand sponsorships fucked and here we are.) In theory, this now meant anyone anywhere could upload a video that could also be viewed by anyone anywhere or, hopefully, everyone everywhere. We got to see Charlie bite the finger. We witnessed the evolution of dance. We were drenched in chocolate rain. Who's to say I couldn't have my own fingers chomped for YouTube fame?

Against all odds, I never really tried to start a YouTube channel, and thank god. After we both transferred, my first college roommate and I started a joint channel just for the two of us. We'd leave each other video messages where we'd recount our days, check in, gossip about people still attending the school we left, and wax poetic about the Jonas Brothers. Though it was a very public platform, the videos stayed private. Other than that, I made no big attempts to make comedy sketches or acoustic covers of rap songs as a ploy to Get Famous Quick.

I do currently have a YouTube channel—which I think is technically true of anyone with a Google account—but it's limited to a video résumé and a recording of a book reading. Both are mostly for my own record-keeping and something you needn't use your time trying to find. My time has far passed for YouTube fame, fortune, and videos sponsored by T-Mobile where I write a parody of the 2010 earworm "Like a G6" called "Like a 5G." Instead, I've invested that energy into reflecting deeply on the lives and content of very specific YouTubers.

I often kid myself into thinking I'm watching these videos from an anthropological viewpoint. *Ah, how interesting that so many people are fascinated with the daily routine of the twenty-five-year-old British woman and her pug. Better watch all forty-five minutes to dissect further.* Usually, I am watching out of my own, unexamined fascination. So, in the spirit of showing you things you didn't ask to see—like a toddler bringing a fossilized piece of goose poop to their babysitter—allow me to be your guide on this archaeological dig of some of my favorite YouTube artifacts.

ASMR

I love ASMR. It is my shameful secret that I keep contained to private browsers and the part of my brain that does a little shiver when I hear long fingernails tapping on a wooden surface. ASMR stands for "autonomous sensory meridian response," which, if you are unfamiliar with ASMR as a whole, probably also means nothing to you. It's been described as a pleasant form of paresthesia, which is also a physical sensation derived from no physical contact but one that is uncomfortable and unpleasant. Think, that pins-and-needles feeling you get when your leg has fallen asleep after lying on the couch in the stupidest way possible while you rewatch season one of *Too Hot to Handle*. ASMR is paresthesia's soothing fraternal twin. It's like the tingly feeling you get on your scalp when you get your hair washed at the salon or the pleasant chills you get up your spine when your husband finally agrees to scratch your back in a platonic way for once.

If you ever stumble upon a video and think, *Hmm, could this be ASMR?*, there are a few telltale signs: soft-spoken talking or whispering, gentle hand movements, a sudden rush of guilt despite not doing anything overtly inappropriate. ASMR is a little hard to describe, but you'll know when you hear it. This is made more complex by the many, many subcategories of ASMR videos readily available on YouTube, each meant to elicit the same pleasant shivers in your brain.

There are videos where people just move their hands in a calming way while quietly repeating the noise, "sksksk." There are tapping videos and scratching videos, both with a variety of options should you prefer the sound of someone tapping glass over plastic or scratching velour fabric over cotton. There are typing videos where you can enjoy the sounds of someone tip-tapping away on their keyboard, sometimes accompanied by loud gum chewing to really emphasize the whole school secretary vibe. Though eating sounds are like aural crucifixion to some, they are oddly soothing to others.

And yes, there are lots and lots of eating ASMR videos. Some are focused on foods with a good crunch, some on foods that break apart in a satisfying way, and even more that are best described as . . . um, slurpy? I'm convinced the entire edible honeycomb market is kept afloat by ASMRtists. (Yes, that portmanteau is the unofficial name of people whose videos are dedicated to ASMR. ASMR artists. ASMRtists. Incredible, no notes.) There are also lots of nonsexual role-play videos, which I know sounds like an oxymoron, but they are a large portion of the ASMR videos that exist on YouTube. The roles are usually intentionally mundane: a receptionist checking you into an appointment, someone helping you pick out fabric for your curtains, a person pretending to give you a haircut. Sometimes they delve into fantasy roles, with ASMRtists dressed as elves, witches, fairies, mermaids, a girlfriend who will listen to you.

As anyone who also enjoys ASMR will insist, it's not inherently sexual. IT'S NOT, OKAY?! Like everything else on the internet, there are readily available borderline pornographic ASMR videos. But many are not filmed and posted with the intention to get you horny. However, I'll be the first to admit that the bridge from ASMR to NSFW is fairly self-explanatory and not nearly as far a stretch as whatever twisted path you need to go down to find, say, anime porn featuring the parents on *Arthur*.

It doesn't help that one of the main words associated with ASMR is *tingles*. "Tingles" sounds perverted, and "shivers" is only a tiny bit better. Describing ASMR also doesn't help prove its lack of inherent sexuality. *So, this video is just a pretty lady pretending to brush my hair and whispering unintelligibly. This one is a different pretty lady tapping her acrylics on an iPad and smiling.*

Another common theme among ASMR videos is women. The vast majority of ASMRtists are women. Nice, comforting women with soft, sweet voices. Pretty women with gorgeously manicured nails. Young women pretending to be a mean cashier berating you at a Starbucks—"Getting lightly bullied" is its own sect of ASMR role-play. Many of the women, especially those who run the most popular ASMR channels, are some combination of hyperfeminine, maternal, and girl-next-door.

I've tried to listen to male ASMRtists and I can't. They ick me out. A man I don't know whispering in my ear isn't soothing; it's a threat. It doesn't give me "tingles" unless you're talking about how my finger would feel after I maced this strange man. The reasons female ASMRtists dominate the space seem fairly obvious and indicative of the culture at large. Women are seen as caretakers, as inherently soft and gentle, as easy to look at, as people designed to cater to you, as someone you wouldn't immediately punch if they came up to you and softly asked, "Is it all right if I play with your hair?"

The audience, on the other hand, seems to be a mix of everyone. Based on what comes up when you search "ASMR," the intended audience of these videos runs the gamut: lonely single men; women who just want to zone out; students who need something to listen to while studying; people seeking something meditation-adjacent; people looking to relax, ease anxiety, get help falling asleep; people who miss having a parental figure, a sibling, someone close enough to them to quietly ask how they're doing.

Some of the reasons ASMR is comforting are also the reasons it can feel sad. Maybe that's just a thing I feel because I am a member of its audience and am often a deeply sad person. The themes present in many ASMR videos imply a level of isolation, a lack of intimate relationships in the viewer's life. If you don't have someone in your immediate vicinity who will listen intently, pat your back, and reassure you, there are hundreds if not thousands of ASMRtists ready to provide that for you unconditionally.

When I watch an ASMR video, I inevitably start thinking about what kind of ASMR channel I would start. (My ego is relentless!) I'll wonder what my specific niche would be should writing fall through or I submit to the part of my brain convinced I'd make bank doing tippy-tappy videos. I'll think about how I'd probably start off not showing my face but eventually end up filming videos with my whole head in frame. I'll posit that I'd probably be hesitant and uncomfortable and later, a little too comfortable. I'll wonder whether this new career path would hurt my job chances elsewhere, should I want to go back to doing something boring like writing. This is the same conversation I have in my brain when I think about selling foot pics online.

Sometimes, when I'm feeling extra maternal, I'll do a little in-person ASMR session with Ava. I'll gently scratch her ears and brush out her fur, both with a bit more care and intention than when I'm doing those things rotely, reflexively. I'll tell her she's so good and so small and ask if she knows those things about herself. I'll pretend to do her nails, inspect her paws. She usually falls asleep and I usually end up sleepy as well.

I suppose that's what I enjoy most about ASMR videos—the space they provide for a little bit of quiet and rest, especially on a platform known for clickbait thumbnails and videos with titles like "PRANKING MY GIRLFRIEND BY PRETENDING I POISONED HER WHOLE FAMILY (emotional)." There are so few places, both online and off, designed to make you feel calm, relaxed, tended to. There are even fewer that seem personal, intentional, and without some ulterior motive to get you to buy a bamboo yoga mat or a stinky tea that ends up giving you diarrhea.

In that sense, I'm fine with keeping relatively quiet about my love of ASMR. I suppose it's only fitting.

MUKBANGS

I guess a recurring theme among videos I like is "things that sound like they could easily be made pornographic, but I swear that's not why I'm watching." With that in mind, let's talk about mukbangs. These are videos where someone rambles a bit or answers questions while eating what is often an unreasonable amount of food. It's a trend that started in South Korea and has seeped to all parts of the World Wide Web. Sometimes, a mukbang consists of a person talking about their day while eating lunch or dinner. Occasionally, that person is sampling a new menu item or eating something they've never tried before from a fast-food restaurant. Usually, the person is eating a lot of food. Like "one slice of every cheesecake on the Cheesecake Factory's novel of a menu" a lot.

My favorite way to eat a meal at home is on the couch while watching TV. It's like dinner and a show for every meal. Whatever I'm eating, be it a light snack or a multicourse meal, it must be paired with some form of media. There are two exceptions: I'm having dinner with friends or Riley and I haven't seen each other most of the day and uh, okay, fine, I guess we can talk while we eat. Otherwise, I must have all my senses engaged at once. This is probably a product of constant overstimulation, and I'm probably melting my brain in some way, but you know what? I don't care! I just want to eat my Kraft mac and cheese and find out what's going on with Dawson and his creek. Also, I swear this method makes me enjoy whatever I'm eating more. I would probably house an entire head of lettuce if you plopped me down in front of a television and turned on reruns of *Boy Meets World*.

Watching a mukbang while I'm eating a meal is another level of bliss. It's like I'm eating with a friend who has a bunch of really good gossip to share, and I just get to chomp and listen. The only thing that would make it better is if I somehow got to eat the same thing as the person doing the mukbang. Actually, I could very easily do that. I could order Domino's and enjoy it with a stranger who has also ordered Domino's. And Pizza Hut. And Little Caesars. The amount of food people are able to consume in a single mukbang video is truly a sight to behold. It would put Joey Chestnut and his seventy-six stupid hot dogs to shame.

I watch mukbangs in the same way people watch videos of dogs reuniting with their owners who have been overseas. It makes me feel good. Seeing people enjoy food makes my stomach hungry and my heart full.

VLOGS

There are few words more humiliating to say than *vlog*. A combination of the words *video* and *blog*—which itself is a portmanteau of *web log*—the vlog is essentially a home movie you put on YouTube for all the world to see. Some YouTubers create a vlog channel separate from their main channel. The vlog channel is usually slightly less polished. Videos have fewer edits, a little less performance. They're not in a home studio, set up in front of a camera. Rather than focusing on one specific topic (e.g., "Haul of What I Bought at Target" or "Trying on Amazon Baby Clothes"), vlogs are usually just a video diary of what someone did during the day.

There are some YouTubers whose whole thing is vlogs. (Your Jake Pauls, your David Dobriks.) However, their vlogs are of a completely different flavor than these daily peeks into a person's everyday life. It's like comparing mild salsa and a handful of ghost peppers. They're similar, in theory, but consuming the latter will often leave a bad taste in your mouth and have you asking, *Why did I think that was a good idea?* These kinds of vlogs consist of staged stunts, manufactured reactions, and video titles like "Surprising My Friends with a Porn Star Who Shoots Fire Out Her Coochie (not clickbait!)." They're high energy, often full of quick cuts and yelling. They're meant to elicit the feeling of, *Wow, their life looks nuts.* What often isn't shown is the production cost that goes into a video like that, the amount of planning and forethought necessary to just come upon "An Abandoned Treasure Chest?! 1 Million Likes and I'll Open It Up!"

I don't know what it is about a person simply filming what they do in a day, unproduced, unedited, but if I see the words *daily routine* or *just a boring weekend*, I cannot help but click. A trip to Trader Joe's and a Target run? Sure! A day of baking and gardening? Yes! Give me half an hour of you talking about this podcast you're listening to while you make dinner. Give me a multipart series where you organize your bedroom closet, stopping occasionally to ask the future audience, "Do you think I should keep this?" It's like the most mundane form of voyeurism and I cannot get enough.

A commonality among many of these vlogs, especially the ones with a significant number of views, is they feature people (usually young, white women) who subtly reveal that they have a lot of money. Often, that money comes from paid posts on Instagram or brands who sponsor the very vlogs you're watching. An Everlasting Gobstopper of video consumption. Despite whatever they chose to title their videos, rarely are the people featured in the vlogs individuals I would describe as "regular." They've made a career by showing people a peek into their lives. They get paid to let us look inside their house, at what they eat and wear, where they shop, how they exercise, who they hang out with and date. People will film themselves when they cry, when they're mad, when they're confused and trying to sort something out, when they're at their most vulnerable.

Or are they? Is it still vulnerability when there is a paycheck on the other side? Does it matter if all this closeness and intimacy is authentic, or does it only matter that it is perceived that way?

Vlogs are middle ground between my quiet fascination with ASMR and the overstimulation that is a mukbang. They're all at once boring and busy, organic and manufactured, accessible and entirely unattainable. If nothing else, they delude me into thinking there is an audience who would gladly tune in to time-lapse videos of me staring at my computer, my phone, and then my dog for hours on end. A humiliating admission! And sure, the word *vlog* is embarrassing, but often, so is life.

One of the strangest, most pleasant places on the internet is Astronaut.io, a website that shows a stream of YouTube videos that have no views. You'll see about eight seconds of a class presentation, someone zooming in on the seams of a dress, a dressage competition, and then the video will switch to another previously unseen video. It feels both extremely public and incredibly intimate. You'll feel like you're seeing something you weren't meant to, but then, you remember, these are all videos someone put up for someone's consumption, even if they thought it'd only be their own. Watching them feels like when you accidentally walked in on someone in the bathroom, but they're just washing their hands. You're not seeing anything out of the ordinary, nothing too private. But it still feels like you stumbled on someone's secret.

It is from there where I would pick the very last YouTube video I'd ever watch; it'd be one of the randomized eight-second clips from that website. This is, in part, because I'm far too indecisive to pick for myself. How would I choose between someone trying everything on Taco Bell's breakfast menu and a thirty-five-minute loop of someone tapping on a piece of cork in a satisfying way? How would I pick between the forty-five-minute vlog of Christmas 2019 and the fifty-five-minute farmers market haul? Spoiled for choice! Instead, I will let the little algorithm decide for me; it only seems fitting. Plus, there is nothing that so perfectly encapsulated what YouTube is, was, or could be than this site aggregating all these lost videos. If I could only feast my eyes on YouTube once more, I would want it to be one of these unintentional pieces of art, these gorgeous short films. I want to be bored and surprised, amazed and unintrigued, see the most public version of the private self.

DON'T MEET
YOUR ENEMIES

Is James Van Der Beek mad at me? is a real thought I
have had before. While my obsessively anxious brain has come up
with plenty of imagined encounters in which I address Dylan Mc-
Dermott as Dermot Mulroney or meet Gwyneth Paltrow and call
her "goop," I have actually met James Van Der Beek.

At a 2015 fundraising event, *Dawson's Creek* himself, along with
celebrities like Olivia Wilde, Selena Gomez, and Paul Rudd, graced
a Kansas City–area bowling alley to throw heavy balls for charity.
The company I worked for at the time sponsored a bowling team and
I was blessed/cursed with the opportunity to stand near hot famous
people with a handful of my coworkers. It was a fever dream from
which I could not wake up.

With the bravery of one Bloody Mary, I decided that if there
were ever a time I'd get to talk to somebody famous, this was it. I
was too afraid to approach Selena Gomez or Olivia Wilde because
I think if I ever stood next to someone that hot, I would turn into
goo like one of Ursula's cursed polyp people from *The Little Mer-
maid*. I did get a picture with Paul Rudd, which is not a knock on
Paul Rudd's hotness but proof that the Bloody Mary was working.

Bolstered by the power of vodka and a single photo with Paul Rudd, I thought I'd go talk to James Van Der Beek.

Did I want a picture? Obviously. But I also wanted to pretend like I was a cool normie. I wasn't one of those embarrassing people who sees a celebrity only as a potential photo op for Instagram so former classmates can see and be like, "Oh, damn, *Is Mia dating Dawson's Creek?*" So I walked up to James Van Der Beek, probably shook his hand, and tried to strike up a conversation. I can feel your butthole clenching in discomfort as you read this. Please know I'm sorry, and keep clenching because I'm not done yet.

I think I thanked him for being there? Not that I had any say in the matter or involvement in organizing the event. But it only seemed polite for me, a plebe, to express gratitude to James Van Der Beek, a '90s god, for his mere presence. I asked if he had taken part in the charity event before—I don't remember his answer because I was too busy thinking about something, anything to ask him next. "Have you been to Kansas City before?" I asked. Again, who's to say how he answered. After standing in silence for a second or a minute or three years, I asked for a picture. He obliged, I thanked him again and proceeded to spend the rest of the event as far away from him as possible.

Could it have gone worse? Absolutely. There are plenty of alternate universes in which I call him Dawson to his face or ask how often he FaceTimes Michelle Williams or think it's a good idea to regurgitate the plot of every episode of *Don't Trust the B—— in Apartment 23*, only stopping to apologize for it being canceled. Still, after our brief encounter, I spent an inordinate amount of time wondering whether James Van Der Beek thought I was annoying. My brain would not slow down on the matter. Did he think it was dumb of me to have asked if he'd even been to Kansas City, a place whose claim to fame is, "there are two of me and only one is in Kansas"? Was he disappointed that I so quickly made it clear that all I really wanted was to ask for a picture? Did he think my hair looked good? Have I now joined the amorphous blob of other complete strangers who have approached him with overfamiliarity?

Also, I've never seen a single episode of *Dawson's Creek*. Not one. Still, it broke my brain ever so slightly to meet him in real life. Standing that close to someone whose IMDb page you've frequented feels like a fever dream. It wasn't impossible to separate James, the actor on television, from James, the person standing in front of me—it just wasn't easy. And it made my brain hurt trying.

• •

I have very little desire to meet any celebrities in real life. If given the chance to invite any five famous people to dinner, I would pass, thanks. I would rather eat every meal off the floor for the rest of my life than have to try to figure out what the fuck I'd say to Lucy Liu as we wait for our soup. What do you even order as a shared appetizer for yourself and the *Power Rangers*? If anything, I'd love to arrange a dinner party of famous people and observe from a table over. I am giddy from the idea of overhearing Nicole Kidman make small talk with the youngest brother from *Home Improvement*.

I know you're not supposed to meet your heroes. I know that the idea of a person, especially a person who is famous, will rarely be an exact match for who they actually are. There are Reddit threads and gossip blogs dedicated to validating the belief that all the people you admire from afar are never as great as they seem. There is a story for most any celebrity you love in which they are significantly more human than you'd hoped.

Not even the kindest soul is exempt—I mean, did you watch the documentary on Mr. Rogers? Were you not disappointed to hear

Mr. Fred "It's You I Like" Rogers discouraged his castmate Officer Clemmons from publicly coming out as gay? The story is, of course, more complex than that. Rogers told Clemmons that he, personally, was fine with Clemmons's sexuality. But "if you're going to be on the show as an important member of The Neighborhood, you can't be out as gay . . . I wish it were different, but you can't have it both ways. Not now anyway." That's devastating for a million different reasons, one of them being the unsurprising reality that Mr. Rogers wasn't ready to publicly combat homophobia. I do think it's a bit ironic given that the Kingdom of Make-Believe is absolutely queer canon and among the most diverse casts PBS, or any network for that matter, has ever had. Henrietta Pussycat is an incredible name for a drag queen. Who doesn't see themselves in a beaver named Corny who makes rocking chairs? Other members of this hyperinclusive kingdom include Hilda Dingleboarder, Yo-Yo LaBelle, Lady Elaine Fairchilde, X the Owl, Old Goat, New Goat, and Queen Saturday. Puppets are basically a drag show for your hands.

Don't worry, I have no interest in dissecting all the ways in which Mr. Rogers is #problematic. I am not canceling his offshoot show *Daniel Tiger's Neighborhood*, though his PBS brethren *Caillou* is on thin ice. We are all a product of our respective times and have the potential to grow and change along with the rest of the world, and I bet Mr. Rogers would have made a fair and entertaining judge on *RuPaul's Drag Race*.

Still, the reminder that those we idolize and deify are just mortal skin sacks like the rest of us is disappointing. And I'd be lying if I said I wasn't interested in knowing whether Ariana Grande is nice to waiters, if Donald Glover waits his turn at a four-way stop. Are the Olsen twins too successful to be bothered with saying "thank you" when someone holds the door for them? Does the Pepsi Girl tip well? At what point does talent outweigh social niceties?

I think most people know or at least know of one person who is seen as so good in their respective field that their shitty behavior is excused. If you are smart enough, talented enough, funny enough, good enough at music or sports or math or being professionally hot, at some point, the world at large unofficially agrees that you don't need to be nice. Or, at least, you can get away with occasionally being terrible. If I found out that Mariah Carey rejected a picture with a fan, it wouldn't make me want to stop listening to "Emotions" altogether. Were I to hear that he was a little rude to an extra on set, I don't think I'd drool over Michael B. Jordan any less.

In that sense, I can see why people excuse the actions of a person they admire. I understand the instinct to say, "Yeah, okay, *but . . .*" when you hear that someone you've looked up to and loved did a terrible thing. It is strange, though, how excellence in one area of life can seemingly be more important than how someone makes other people feel, more valuable than their willingness to participate in human decency.

Perhaps this is why it hurts worse to find out someone whose niceness has been celebrated turns out to be a secret asshole. The allegations against Ellen DeGeneres's toxic workplace were painfully ironic given her whole "Be Kind" branding. Joss Whedon allegedly being awful to the women in his life stung more knowing how loudly he was lauded for being an exemplary male feminist and creating strong female characters on-screen. As if performing niceness is only tolerable when able to do so for a profit.

The desire to separate art from the artist is exhausting. It quickly derails legitimate criticism and conversations that started with sentences like, "Have you heard about the latest Bad Thing another famous man did?" The willingness to culturally excuse bad behavior to preserve potential success is so often reserved for shitty rich men. It's not a courtesy typically extended to members of historically less-powerful groups, to people labeled "bitchy" or "hard to work with." Sure, she's vocally very talented and her music's fun to listen to, but I heard that her show rider asks for a bowl of only green M&Ms! Sure, he assaulted dozens of people, but his show changed the landscape of television!

How cool of a movie do you have to make for "assault of a minor" to be secondary to your job title? How funny a joke do you have to tell for your audience to ignore how often you showed colleagues your dick? How talented a swimmer do you need to be for your future to outweigh that of the person you raped? Don't meet your heroes, but if you do and they turn out to be the villain, you better find a way to change the narrative quickly.

• •

At that same 2015 charity event, there was another celebrity whose behavior I've thought too much about over the years. He paid attention to me in a way that was uncomfortable but not outright alarming. It started as overly familiar ribbing, loudly yelling to/at me from too far away. At one point, a group of people in the bowling lane over asked to take a picture with him. My coworkers and I moved out of the way so as to not make an unintentional cameo in the background of the photo. As the other group was gathering to take the picture, the actor kept backing up until he intentionally bumped into me, squishing me between his back and a table. He jokingly told me to get out of the way knowing that I couldn't move. The group took the photo and I probably laughed a little to diffuse the situation. Somewhere on some Instagram, my ponytail is in the back of this celebrity photo op.

Again, I wouldn't characterize this as capital b "Bad." And nothing he did was really that surprising given his personal brand as an actor—in this instance, the art and the artist were one and the same.

But it was noticeable enough that my boss said, "Do you want to go to a different table so [redacted] leaves you alone?" Earlier, I had worried that James Van Der Beek thought I sounded stupid, that Selena Gomez's hotness would melt my face off. Now, I was being asked if a famous man was bothering me. The line between human person and celebrity person felt both completely impenetrable and at the same time flimsy and nonexistent. Would I have tolerated this kind of weird attention from someone who didn't have ten million Instagram followers and some other famous friends?

Eventually, he stopped shouting my name and bumping into me when I stopped responding altogether. At the end of the event, he came up to me, shook my hand, and said it was so nice to meet me. I probably said it was nice to meet him, too.

I don't really know what to do with that encounter in my mind. Maybe it just validates the fact that I wasn't a huge fan of his to begin with. I guess it is okay to not be a fan of the art or the artist. Or maybe I hold it with me as personal proof of some greater problem, as evidence of how easy it is for celebrated men to do whatever they please. I don't know if the encounter even bears repeating, but I do think about it when I hear his name, when people talk about how famous men behave in private. I guess, if nothing else, it reaffirmed that James Van Der Beek *was* kind when I asked for a photo too soon or not soon enough, that this other actor *was* rude and felt entitled to my attention, and that I *was* thinking too much about whether I am part of an amorphous blob. I am, and that's okay.

After that encounter, I started thinking about what I'd do if I ever encountered a famous person I didn't like again. It is, at least, a little more fun than panicking about meeting celebrities I love. What would I say to the actor from the charity event on the very slim chance that we crossed paths once more? I'd probably just shake his hand and say that it's so nice to meet him.

PART 4

Good Girl, Bad Bitch

I'M THE BAD GUY

Let's say I'm the villain of the story. We'll say this because it's true. You know I am the villain because I am sharp and pointy, quiet but not in a good way, and the music goes *dun dun DUN* when I walk into frame.

If it helps, I'm a woman. Just kidding, I know it helps. It makes me softer, less threatening. How will I catch you while wearing these heels? Are you sure I'm not just on my period? At the same time, it's scarier. A lifetime of being made to believe I am too weak to punch walls or start a lawn mower or hold office or open jars.

And yet, I am bad.

What is the scariest thing a woman can do? Talk too much? Disagree? Share your unprompted nude picture with the group chat? Ask why you didn't do the dishes? Text when you're out too late? Wake up early and make coffee when you hoped she'd leave? Find where you hide your browser history? Discover you've had another family all along? Move in too soon? Love you too quickly? Cry without reason? Ignore your jokes? Laugh at you? Say no? Laugh at you *while* saying no?

Men are made to be monstrous. They are shaped into statues, told to speak up, be stronger, be bigger, to inhale until they puff up like an upside-down triangle, to take up as much space as a bus. Their skin grows thick to keep in things like worry, fear, sadness, nurturing, gentleness, servitude, the desire to be cared for, and protein powder. Holding tears in builds muscle quicker. Monstrosity is in their nature and their nurture. After all, boys will be boys. We all know the scary things men can do. It's more surprising when they choose otherwise.

Do I look like someone who's hurt people before? Is it scarier if you don't know? I know plenty of women who have hurt plenty of people. They've perfected death stares, cutting between the soft parts of strangers' fingers after the stranger tried to interlace their hands with hers. They've swapped spiked drinks and snuck away to leave the men to sleep in solitude. I heard about a woman who ate an apple and made a man kiss her lifeless body to wake her up. I heard about another woman who ate an apple and damned humanity. I also know a woman who ate an apple as a snack and pretended it was as satisfying as handfuls of cake and expensive jewels. When it comes to women, eating apples is a red flag.

What if I told you I've done something much worse?

I haven't even told you my name, and you want to know the worst things I've done? Well, you're lucky, because I don't have a name. Women don't have names, they have husbands. In the Bible, her given name is Lot's wife. Women don't have names, they have warnings. Sirens are called sirens for a reason. Women don't have names, they have relationships: mother, daughter, friend's sister, First Lady, grandma, grandpa's girlfriend, dad's new wife. The only time women have names is in secret, but you already suspected that. And you don't want to know the names we have for you.

So, do you want to know what I've done? Too bad, I'm telling you anyway. (Talking out of turn is the second-worst thing I've done.) Years and years ago, I found a spot in the middle of the woods that was cleared in a perfect circle—no grass or plants or flowers or dead birds or bear shit. Just a circle of dirt surrounded by a ring of trees so tall their tops could have had huge faces and I would never have known. When I stood in the dirt circle, looking up at the sky then back down at the ground, I could tell no person had ever been there before. The earth was completely untouched. It seemed the circle was just there by coincidence or God or demons or math. I guess I've never really thought about why there was a circle or how it came to be. I just saw it and felt like I wanted to dig. So I did.

I often do things without asking first. That's how you know I'm bad. Medusa didn't ask whether her hair looked good like that. Witches don't check whether their child-luring candy houses are up to code. I didn't even think about asking if I could dig. I didn't pray about it or ask the sky or just shout really loudly, "Anyone saving this big dirt circle for something?"

I pushed the dirt around with my foot and noticed the topsoil was soft. So I knelt down and took a scoop of loose dirt into my hand. It was so much softer than I thought it'd be. It felt like snow that didn't melt and wasn't cold. Or sand that wasn't too dry. At first, I didn't try to dig—or didn't try to look like I was trying to dig. I picked up a scoop of dirt, sifted it through my hands, and then set it aside. I did this again and again. Soon, there was a small indent in the middle of the circle about the size and depth of my fist. I thought about covering it back up. It would have been easy to do and would have made it look brand-new or at least how it looked when I'd found it. But instead, I decided to keep digging. I was curious how deep the soft soil went, and it also felt good to dig. So I did.

That first day, I dug with my hands and then, when it got deeper, I used my entire arms. Soon—or maybe after a really long time, it's kind of hard to tell in the woods—I decided I was done for the day and went back home.

But I kept going back to the circle to dig. The next time, I brought a shovel with me so it'd go faster, I guess. I wasn't really in any rush, but it seemed like the natural, more efficient thing to do. Again, I dug for a while. Again, all the dirt I found was as soft as that topsoil. Again, I grew tired and eventually returned home. I got into a routine that didn't have any real schedule so I guess that isn't a routine, is it? I'd go home for days or weeks or hours or years, but then, sometimes out of nowhere, I'd think about the hole. I'd work and eat and cry and sleep and scream and love and fight, but I'd always find myself back at the hole. At first, I called it "the circle" but now it feels wrong to call it anything except "the hole."

A few times I thought about bringing someone with me, but what was I going to say? *Do you want to come touch this soft dirt I found? I've been digging a big hole, would you like to see?* Having to say that is worse than digging a hole alone in the woods. If it's still happening, if I'm still digging the hole, is it the worst thing I've *done*? I guess it'll be the worst thing I'll have done one day. For now, I guess it's just the talking-out-of-turn thing.

Yes, I am still digging. I have been for hundreds of years. I'm sure you don't believe me—women do like to lie, especially about their age. But you can't tell how old I am, can you? You can't tell if my hair has been dyed to look less gray, if my eyes have been outlined to seem older, if my body looks good for my age or mature for my age. Either way, it precedes my age. I know that this all makes me even more threatening. Is being seen with me a crime or just embarrassing?

The way women become evil starts with the way they look. It starts with making our hair seem softer than it is, our eyelashes longer than they could ever have grown on their own. Then, it grows into making our eyes bigger, our skin softer, our cheeks so shiny it hurts to look at our face. You know the evil is spreading when we can make ourselves smell like fruit and springtime, like home and lemon, like the babysitter, the mother, the wife, the daughter. You didn't notice the dirt under my nails. I painted them so you couldn't see.

Maybe you think digging a hole doesn't seem that bad, but we both know it can't be good. Does the Earth want to be uncovered? Dug into? Scooped out and left hollow?

Maybe, you think, part of the reason it's bad is because I feel no remorse. You're right. I don't care if it's bad. I don't care if someone else wanted to dig there, if it wasn't meant to be dug into at all. I'm not bothered by the idea that I am unearthing something terrible, which I most certainly am. You can't dig this deeply without letting something out.

If I started singing right now, would you find it funny? What if I sang really softly without any music? I've heard that there is a specific pitch you can sing that drives people mad or makes them soil themselves or sob uncontrollably. Maybe that pitch is so high you don't know when you're hearing it. And when you realize, it's already too late.

I don't know when the soil stopped being soft, but it doesn't feel the same as it used to. The past few times I went, the bottom of the hole felt cold and wet. When I grabbed a handful and tried to look at it, it just crumbled. It didn't sift through my fingers like it used to. It didn't feel special or secret like it had before. If that was meant to stop me from digging, it didn't work. If anything, that made me want to dig more.

Would it make you feel better to know that I wasn't always the bad guy? Maybe you can attribute my madness to my mother, my classmates, a stranger in an alley, a friend turned foe?

It'd be easier if that were true. If there was a time where I didn't feel the need to dig. If there was a version of myself that would've left the earth alone. Maybe you hope that I'm a sheep in wolf's clothing, that somewhere, deep down, I can be saved or changed or that, at least, I have an excuse.

Then, you could say, "I mean, her mother *was* eaten by a hole."

Or "When she was younger, she was always covered in dirt" so you should have seen the signs or kept me from returning to the things that led to digging. Maybe I never had a hole growing up or I was surrounded by so many holes my life was fated to be riddled with them forever. Or you could say, "Actually, she herself is a hole so it's rooted in self-hatred. By digging, what she means is that she wants to dig into herself." Maybe it's been the hole all along? Maybe I was fine until I started digging? Maybe there was something hidden in the hole that got into me. Maybe that's a privilege reserved for men: to change and be changed.

If you're wondering what my family thinks about the hole, don't worry. I don't have any family. Or if I did they're long gone. Or I killed them or they killed themselves or they were just a dream all along. Truthfully, I don't really remember. It certainly seems like I should have a family, be somebody's daughter, someone's mother. It seems like I would have thought about having children at some point. But who would have let me be a mother? Who would have wanted me enough to make me one?

How about this: If I did have a child, you can imagine her as a daughter. She can be gentle and sweet and look like your daughter or your niece or mother as a baby or yourself as a baby or a baby you saw once that made you say, "Aww!" The daughter will grow up with me or away from me. Either way, she grows and grows and doesn't dig. She saw what digging did to her mother and doesn't want the same for herself. She knows she shouldn't want the same. People ask if she ever tried to stop her mother from digging, if anyone tried to stop her. They'll ask if we talked about the digging at home or if we pretended it didn't happen. Eventually, they stop asking about her mother. The daughter grows up to be someone else's mother. Everyone is amazed at how far she made it, how she was able to keep herself from repeating her mother's habits, how she was able to stop herself from digging. Then, one day, the daughter will see a small patch of dirt in the middle of an otherwise perfect field. She'll put her hand on the soil to see if it's soft. And, one day, when her own daughter asks about her grandmother, she'll think about this patch.

I'm starting to forget what the soft soil felt like, what made me start digging in the first place. I'm not sure if that even matters anymore. Maybe one day we can decide if it does. For now, I am going to keep digging.

GOOD GIRL, BAD BITCH

do not radiate Bad Bitch energy. I am a nervous bitch. I am a scaredy bitch. I am a bitch who looks both ways before crossing the street and will mouth *SORRY* to cars if the light turns green while I'm still in the crosswalk. I'm a bitch who turns the music down when I'm trying to figure out if I missed my exit on the highway. I'm a bitch who does her taxes early, a bitch with a favorite flavor of LaCroix. I'm a bitch with an in-box full of emails from my bank, each with a new link to reset my forgotten password. I'm that bitch who knows all the words to Nicki Minaj's verse in "Monster" because I am also that bitch who looked up the lyrics and practiced. I'm an approachable bitch, a disarming bitch, a bitch who will roll over and show you the pink of my belly if I sense even a whiff of confrontation. I'm a bitch who would cry if you ever called me a bitch in real life.

In theory, I'd love to be a Bad Bitch. From what I understand, a Bad Bitch does whatever she pleases. She takes no shit. She's independent, self-confident, and unapologetically assertive. She responds to internet trolls by saying things like, "I will dog walk you." She can destroy your spirit and ruin your life with the shake of a single ass cheek. She will humiliate those who've never tasted humility, shame the truly shameless. If you look at a Bad Bitch the wrong way, she'll telepathically destroy your credit score. A Bad Bitch doesn't care. A Bad Bitch pays her own bills and drives her own car. A Bad Bitch quits her job just to spend her days driving around in that car, windows down, sunglasses on, cackling into the sunset. What do Bad Bitches do for a living? Babe, being a Bad Bitch is a full-time career. Bad Bitches break up with their boyfriend. They'll break up with your boyfriend. A Bad Bitch is in a relationship with herself.

She is the most of whatever people don't want or don't expect her to be. She doesn't care what anyone thinks of her appearance. This is, in part, because she knows she looks good. A Bad Bitch is the definition of "looking good." She's got money but wasn't born into wealth. No one with generational wealth can be a Bad Bitch—this is as close to wealth redistribution as we're going to get for right now. She's horny as fuck but that's none of your business unless she tells you it is. Her ass is fat for her and her alone.

In some ways, the Bad Bitch is the Cool Girl reimagined under the female gaze. She, like the Cool Girl, exists in contradictions, but a Bad Bitch revels in the dissonance. A Cool Girl is hot in a disarming way, fun in a bro-ish way. She gets along better with guys, which she's already told you twice. A Cool Girl is down for whatever. She's just chill like that. She's akin to the hypothetical Guy's Girl, eager to assimilate to the men around her, desperate to distinguish herself from *those* girls. The ones who are overly emotional, overly feminine, three-dimensional. A Bad Bitch, on the other hand, is not concerned with seeming "chill." She gives zero fucks, and yes, she can quantify her fucks. She's not one of *those* girls. The ones who care what anyone thinks, let alone *a man*. A Cool Girl likes whatever you like. You will love whatever a Bad Bitch loves.

To be a fully realized Bad Bitch, you probably have to know with certainty that you're a Bad Bitch, right? You probably have to be able to identify Bad Bitch behavior as it's happening, to call yourself as such without hesitating. I'm also guessing Bad Bitches don't use words like *probably* and end sentences asking, "Right?" There are times I've been a Bad Bitch in hindsight, which doesn't qualify me for full-time Bad Bitchery, but I'll take what I can get.

Against all odds, one of the times I flirted with being a Bad Bitch was in middle school. I had a math teacher who for reasons still unknown did not like me. (I was used to indifference from authority figures, but I was far too afraid of getting in trouble to do anything with the intent to make an adult dislike me. So this was new.) Though it's entirely contradictory to who I am as a person, having a nemesis is a great starting point for a Bad Bitch education.

My teacher was convinced I was making fun of her on a regular basis, and I learned this after she kept me after class one time to confront me about it. "I noticed that when I put my hand to my chin, you did the same thing," she said, clearly believing she'd caught me doing something punishable. I can't remember how to multiply polynomials, but I would testify in court with total confidence that my prealgebra teacher accused me of putting my hand to my chin the same way she did. She also said she heard me whisper things when she turned her back to the whiteboard and could tell I was the "ringleader" of second-hour prealgebra, goading my classmates to quietly mock her along with me. The idea that anyone would ever describe my thirteen-year-old self as a "ringleader" is hilarious. I was walking around with Nair chemical burns on my upper lip and hoping that smiling counted as class participation. There was nary a ring that I would have been capable of leading.

This isn't to say I wasn't an asshole in middle school because I absolutely was. Like many teens, I experimented with the limits of just how foul I could be upon going through puberty. I screamed at my mom. I bullied people over AOL Instant Messenger and said rancid things about people I considered friends. I acted in ways that were awful and inexcusable, especially if I believed it would make hotter, cooler people pay attention to me. (It rarely did.) Thinking of the things I did and said when I was twelve or thirteen still makes me nauseous with shame and regret. For the most part, I wasn't a Bad Bitch; I was just bad.

While I feel certain that I never made fun of this teacher in her presence, it's not unlikely that, outside of class, I joined in if other kids were saying the kinds of things kids say about middle school teachers they don't like. But because of my own cowardice, I know this was never done face-to-face if only through motivation to maintain the appearance that I was a Good Kid.

Good Kids behave. They are quiet, a little scared, and have unwavering respect for anyone more than eighteen months older than them. Good Kids clean up after themselves. They clean up after others. Really Good Kids don't make messes in the first place. They're home before curfew—if they are not given one, they'll determine a reasonable hour for themselves. Good Kids don't speed up when the light turns yellow. They do the reading, go to class, tell the teacher that they forgot to check their assignments from last night.

I don't remember exactly what I said when my teacher confronted me. I'm guessing I tried to convince her I didn't do whatever she thought I did. I was probably quiet and nervous. But I don't think I apologized—a rarity for someone who would say, "No, sorry, that was my bad" were someone to hit me with their car. Not saying "sorry" to a teacher who mistakenly accused me of mocking them is about as close to Bad Bitchery as I got in my adolescence.

Because Bad Bitches must come with a soundtrack, the only other time I dabbled in being a Bad Bitch as a teenager came during—this is painful for me to even write—my singer-songwriter phase. I listened to Michelle Branch on repeat, learned three chords on the guitar, and thought, *I could write a song that would ruin a man's life.*

After a summer of being strung along by an unrequited crush, I channeled my seventeen-year-old heartbreak into a song. It had lyrics like, "I wanted what you said that we could be" and "Hey, baby, I wrote you a song, and I used your words so you could sing along." Yes, the song was self-referential; it was a song about a song. Yes, I believed it was my opus and would be a launchpad for stardom. No, it didn't help me get over him. Bolstered by self-delusion and the power of Taylor Swift's budding career, I decided it'd be a good idea to play the song in front of this boy. For someone with a clinical lack of confidence, I sure have a propensity for doing some real bold shit.

One evening, me, this guy—let's call him Joe Jonas—and a couple of our friends planned to hang out at another friend's house. I'd played the song for my friends earlier because of course I did, and afterward, we devised a scheme to "naturally" give me an opportunity to play the song for Joe at some point in the night. Part of this natural plan involved me bringing my guitar with me to this friend's house, something I had never done up until this point. The rest of the plan was something like, "Okay, Mia, I'll ask if you wanna play anything on the guitar, and you'll say 'yes,' and then you'll play the song you wrote." And I thought, *Perfect, a brilliant plan. He'll never suspect a thing.*

When Joe and his friends showed up, the five or six of us all crammed into our friend's bedroom to hang out, as was standard of most early aughts get-togethers in the Midwest. Thus, the plan was set into motion. My friend said the secret code to signal that I should get my guitar. ("Oh, Mia, you brought your guitar.") Then, it was go time.

I'm sure I acted coy like, "But what should I even play??" I probably warmed up with a devastating rendition of "Our Song," as was the tradition of all girls who came of age at the same time as Taylor Swift. Then, it was time to play our song, the one I'd written about Joe.

Have you ever delivered a perfect comeback in conversation instead of just in your head after the fact? Or have you ever parallel parked on your first try with an audience of pedestrians? Or have you ever casually picked up a basketball and made a three with your first shot? Have you ever eaten crème brûlée? Watched fireworks? Felt the magnificence of the ocean? Seen a flower bloom? Playing a "you hurt me" song in front of the person who hurt me felt like that. It was incredible. I have zero recollection of whether I sang well or messed up the words or if the song even sounded good or what his face looked like when I played it, but after I was done, I felt that unmistakable sensation of, *I am the Baddest Bitch*. It was as close to making me cum as this guy ever got.

Later, Joe's friend texted me—this was when phone plans still had a limited number of monthly texts, so you know it was important. He asked, point-blank, if the song I played was about Joe. I lied, like, "No, it was about a different guy who I've been obsessed with for months. You wouldn't know him. He goes to a different school for hot boys." I don't know whether he or Joe believed it; it's still satisfying either way.

As is typical of pseudorelationships in your late teens, Joe and I eventually stopped talking altogether. I moved on to pining after people I passed in my dorm, and he grew weird facial hair. Then, a year or so later, Joe called me out of the blue. He said he'd been talking to a coworker about relationships and realized, in that conversation, that I was his One That Got Away. He didn't use that phrase exactly—he wasn't great with words, which is why I believed I could play a whole-ass song that essentially recounted our months of text messages word for word and assumed he wouldn't suspect a thing. We talked for a bit and the conversation ended with me saying, "Thank you for the opportunity but, unfortunately, I'm going to have to pass at this time."

The only other times I've even been Bad Bitch–adjacent are when I've quit jobs. Driving out of a company parking garage for the last time, signing off from my final work shift, waving goodbye to co-workers like, *Ta-ta, peasants, I'm off to bigger and better things*, even if you have no future plans—these are like a Bad Bitch amuse-bouche. Each a tiny, delicious moment.

But then what?

How do you savor that feeling without going into a full-body panic? How do you say "fuck you" without reflexively following up with an apology? How do you make demands without worrying whether you hurt people's feelings? Make a scene without asking if they need any help cleaning up? Do Bad Bitches not care about those things? Can I be a Bad Bitch while still hoping people like me, while still wanting everyone to think I'm nice?

While I do not emit Bad Bitch vibes, I know I give off Good Girl energy. The kind that would love to meet your mother. The kind that labels you "the marrying type" while you're still a minor. The kind that smiles and nods and waits her turn. Good Girls are boring but easy to be around, nice in a way that borders on unsettling. If Bad Bitches and Cool Girls agree on one thing, it's that Good Girls are annoying.

Honestly, I, too, am skeptical of fellow Good Girls because they seem too good to be true. I have a hard time feeling close to anyone I can't complain with, anyone who has never shown the cracks in their veneer, if there are even any at all. Because, despite being someone desperate for people to see me as good, I know the kinds of things supposedly Good Girls think and say and do, things I've pushed down and excused in myself to keep up appearances.

I know it's not cool to want to be a Good Girl all the time, and I know my desire to be seen as cool is often at odds with my desire to be seen as good. Not good in a genuine, altruistic, or self-examining way. Good in a way that doesn't question or confront and will gladly go along with something if it means people will be comfortable. Good in a way that doesn't challenge authority. Good in a way that doesn't know what "good" means if not in relation to someone else's ideas of obedience.

What if I want to be both a Good Girl and a Bad Bitch? What if I'm actually neither? What if the things I do are neither empowering nor obedient, confident nor actually considerate? What if it's all a ruse to avoid the humiliation of being noticed, the devastating reality that someone will see me as I truly am?

I often worry that I am bad. Not Bad Bitch bad. *Bad* bad. I worry that my generosity is selfish, my kindness is cruel, my confidence is counterproductive, because I worry that I am merely trying to be seen as all these things instead of actually being them. I know part of it comes from a deeply unhealthy view of myself, but another comes from this bigger inability to exist without it feeling performative. I can seem like a Good Girl. I can dabble in playing the part of the Bad Bitch. I can act Cool and Nice and Smart and Good. And I know that no one feels like all those things all the time, but I feel acutely aware of when I am putting on the performance of myself rather than just being myself.

Are you actually nice if a part of your motivation is for others to see you as such? Does it count as self-confidence if it ultimately requires another person's input?

It's telling, at least to me, that the two specific times I felt like a Bad Bitch came at the cost of another person's feelings. It's concerning, at least to me, that I frequently derive self-confidence from other people's perception of who they think I am. I got to pretend to be the Good Girl when my middle school math teacher called me out because she didn't actually catch me doing the bad thing. (Though being unapologetic is Bad Bitch behavior, trying to maintain a feigned image of "goodness" is not.) I got to feel like a Bad Bitch when I sang that song in front of the guy I liked, and again when he tried to rekindle our relationship, because I knew I was doing something in stark contrast to the kind of person he expected me to be.

I wonder what goodness looks like when it isn't celebrated, what self-assurance feels like when it exists independently from anyone else.

I know I'm not the only person who hears "Are there any Bad Bitches in here tonight?" hollers in response, and then continues picking up their friends' empty glasses to take them back to the bar. Even removed from the male gaze, the Bad Bitch is still an ideal just like the Cool Girl before her. She is still unattainable. She is still a performance in herself.

I know I'm not alone in this feeling because why else would there be so many tweets like, "Hot girls have IBS" and "Have you ever met a Bad Bitch who doesn't sweat a lot?" I am among a decent-size population of people who would love to be one of the Bad Bitches in there tonight but, instead, is at home with her pet, zooted off an edible. Because go out? In public? For what??

I am among the Bad Bitches with acne. Bad Bitches with holes in the crotch of their pants and not in a sexy way. Bad Bitches with allergies. Bad Bitches who take naps and bloat easily. Bad Bitches who talk to their dog in a stupid voice and have a compulsion to ask babies how their day was. Bad Bitches with BO. Bad Bitches with underboob sweat. Bad Bitches with unforgivable morning breath. Bad Bitches with clinical depression still figuring out the right balance of medications. Bad Bitches who google "how to be a Bad Bitch" as a joke but still click the links just in case.

Even in admitting that I am not a Bad Bitch, I still want to feel like one. I'd love to pretend that I don't have the instinct to morph into yet another idealized version of myself in order to feel confident, but I feel that pull constantly. Also, I don't want to shake my ass to a song that's like, "I'm a Regular Girl. I do regular shit." Though I'm sure the world would eat that up, too.

Amid the Bad Bitches, the Cool Girls, the Good Girls, the Guy's Girls has emerged a new kind of persona altogether: the Relatable Girl. She's so normal! So self-deprecating! So easy to see yourself in because she is whoever you'd like her to be. Her insecurities are so specific, yet a significant portion of the population can relate. She's so real in a way that is still commodifiable.

As prevalent as feigned confidence and faux kindness have become—can you even imagine a Target display without coffee mugs that say Bo$$ Babe and Be Nice?—so is acknowledging the fact that none of us feel confident and kind all the time. Admitting your humanity—for example, "having a wild Friday night in my pj's drinking wine"—has become its own personality type, its own marketable trait. Me listing the reasons I don't feel like a Bad Bitch, while all true, don't actually come at the cost of vulnerability.

I appreciate that this means we don't have to pretend to be constantly put together, but that also means you really have to dig to be earnest lest you risk sounding trite. Like an Instagram influencer who posts unedited but posed and somehow still performative photos captioned, "This is the real me. Take it or leave it." In truth, the Relatable Girl isn't actually any more human than the Bad Bitch or the Good Girl. More attainable, sure. But she's no more multidimensional. She exists in response to her foremothers. She's a condensed version of our collective desire to be the thing that people like.

Admitting that I don't feel like a Bad Bitch isn't surprising or revolutionary; it's its own little performance. Maybe you don't think I'm cool or confident but maybe you also don't feel that way about yourself. And maybe that will make you like me more.

I worry that, at my worst, all my actions are an act of hoping it will make someone like me more.

Honestly, I think there has only ever been one Bad Bitch in existence. It's this girl, maybe eight or nine years old, from a Vine—a very short viral video if you're too old or young to have heard of Vine. Upon being startled as a joke, the girl doesn't scream or cry or run. She just looks to camera and says, "I'm a Bad Bitch. You can't kill me." Imagine having the kind of confidence that makes you immortal.

APOLOGIES FOR MEN

Has this ever happened to you? You're going about your man business, doing manly things like nodding approvingly at hardwood floors or correcting people on Twitter, when suddenly someone accuses you of a Bad Thing.

You try everything: giving your most sincere shrug, saying "Ha ha, my bad," talking about all the Good Things you've done, reminding them you already said "my bad." Nothing seems to be cutting it, but saying "I'm sorry" just feels too . . . girly. You need something more macho, more masculine . . .

You need Apologies for Men! Finally, saying sorry isn't just for ladies anymore.

Apologies for Men comes in four manly varieties: I Abused My Power (It Is My Curse for Being So Accomplished), I Remember Differently (By That I Mean She's Lying), I Am Stepping Away (Until I Have Enough New Material for a Book or Netflix Special), and Mountain Musk.

Apologies for Men takes the "sorry" out of "I'm sorry" and masks justification as atonement. Layer all four varieties for extra-strength character protection. Apologies for Men comes without those traditionally feminine notes of shame or accountability and is consequence-free as it doesn't include full admission of wrongdoing.

But does it really work? Check out some of the testimonials. The results speak for themselves:

"I finally used Apologies for Men after years of being told I should. People were right: I felt a lot better after using 'I Abused My Power.' Mostly because I got to plug all my shows." —Louis from New York

"I tried Apologies for Men for the first time in 2018. (I had never needed to pay attention to criticism before!) I was even able to exchange my initial apology for a brand-new one. I can proudly say I'm writing this while simultaneously 'Stepping Away.' Can't wait to return refreshed, recharged, and completely unchanged!" —Logan from the internet

"The great thing about Apologies for Men is that it's transferrable. While I've never used it on myself, plenty of people have used Apologies for Men on my behalf, and I've felt a peaceful and entitled creative resolve just the same." —Woody from New York

"I think Apologies for Men is a great thing . . . I would absolutely use Apologies for Men, sometime in the hopefully distant future, if I'm ever wrong." —Anonymous from Mar-a-Lago

Order today! You won't be sorry.

NAUGHTY LIST

When I was in third grade, my parents told me Santa had gotten an email address, so, in lieu of a handwritten letter, I could send my wish list virtually. Of course Santa had internet access in the North Pole. He had flying reindeer and worker elves, why not a Hotmail account?

There were many things I could have asked this mythical wish-granting daddy to do. This was the same year Furbies were the most popular toy. I could have begged Santa to secure a fuzzy bird-gremlin that was powered by batteries / possessed by demons, so my parents wouldn't have to brave the mall to get me one. No, no, eight-year-old me thought, my taste is far more sophisticated. I like BOYS with BAD HAIRCUTS and ZERO INTEREST in ME. So, when the opportunity arose to ask this holiday genie to grant me a gift, I told him exactly what I wanted.

"Dear Santa," I'm assuming the email started. "For Christmas, please make Matt and Bobby like me back." Then, I'm guessing I added "also world peace for all" for good measure, eight-year-old me masking her infinite horniness for male attention with feigned altruism. This was also around the time I cut my Barbie's hair to look like the mom of a different boy I had a crush on. So, if you're wondering whether I've always been this chill, I suppose you have your answer.

I eagerly signed off, hit send, and assumed my message would be flagged as "Urgent!!!" in Santa's in-box.

I never divulged who I liked to anyone other than Santa or my journal. When friends in elementary school would ask who I had a crush on, I would avidly deny liking anyone, even if they'd tell me who they liked. *Me? Like someone???* I'd think, lying to them and myself. No thanks, I'd rather piss my pants on a field trip again than subject myself to something so mortifying.

One time, in elementary school, my aunt figured out who I liked after seeing one (1) holiday choir concert and watching who I interacted with / sang at. In her defense, I have never been known for my subtlety. I expressed my interest primarily through long, unblinking stares. When my aunt gently teased me about it, I reacted by panic crying.

The idea of liking a boy was both humiliating and central to my being. Growing up, I thought that a cool thing about me was that I could name every boy I'd ever liked in chronological order. Sometimes I'd recite the list in my head like a Lou Bega hit: Richie, Michael A., the cartoon Aladdin, Matt B., Matt S., the Blue Power Ranger. By third grade, there were many verses and "Matt" was a common lyric.

Unsurprisingly, my personality was often formed around the boys I liked as well. I was okay with being good at math as long as one of the multiple Matts I liked was also in the advanced math class. I once learned how to play *The Simpsons* theme song on the piano after discovering a boy who I thought was cute liked the show. These are not interesting or unique touchstones of my adolescence. Everyone who's ever liked a boy also went through a phase where they pretended to know hockey or guitar or weed culture as a desperate attempt at connection. "Oh my god, *you* like Wonderwall too? Wow, so crazy!"

It's strange what you remember about your childhood self in hindsight. Things you considered normal or even good as a kid, looking back, were neither normal nor good. In addition to knowing how addicted to male attention I've always been, I remember that, every Christmas, I always secretly peeked at my presents. I mastered the art of quietly tearing open the tiniest corner of a gift, peeking under a bit of paper to see what my parents had lovingly bought and wrapped for me, and taping it shut again. I was not surprised by the Doodle Bear I wanted in first grade. I knew whether my three siblings and I were getting matching Green Bay Packers headbands. (Yes, I occasionally peeked at their gifts as well. And yes, it was the '90s and we lived in Wisconsin.)

Part of the wonder and magic of the holidays is that a wrapped gift can be anything—a lot of KitKats, a Barbie, a handwritten love letter from Matt and Bobby, anything! Still, my desire to know all things always usurped my childhood wonder. Somehow, my parents never caught me.

I needed to spoil these secrets for myself because I've always hated not knowing something that I know other people know—like everyone is in on a secret they won't tell me. Maybe this is why I never wanted to tell anyone about my crushes: I liked having a secret with only myself. I liked the possibility of being liked back but rarely the reality of having to show any kind of vulnerability. Before it is revealed, your crush can lead to anything—being reciprocated tenfold, the beginning to a lifelong romance, a throuple with Matt and Bobby, anything! The best part of having a crush is everything you imagine it could be. The worst part is every other part.

Unlike Doodle Bears or Packers headbands, the Christmas gift I emailed Santa about in third grade was not one I could sneakily unwrap and peek inside. So I waited.

Within a week or so, Santa emailed me back. I refused to let my parents read the response, something I only realize is ironic in hindsight. Covering the screen, I yelled at them to GET OUT of the computer room. When I opened the email, Santa's response was disappointing yet gentle, like a college rejection letter.

"Dear Ms. Mercado, while I appreciate your interest in having multiple relationships at once, making boys like you back is not something I can do."

I remember Santa offering consolation, telling me not to worry about something I could not control. It did little to soothe the fact that I was embarrassed and mad but mostly embarrassed. I'd revealed a secret and Santa was like, "Can't help you there, pal, but thanks for the intel." What if Santa told Matt and Bobby I liked them? Was that something he could do???

The best parts of secrets and surprises are when they are still secrets and surprises, when they could be or mean anything, when they don't require vulnerability or the possibility of rejection. The worst part is nearly always the reveal.

The next year, I learned there is no Santa Claus. A friend told me casually one day, like, "So you know how Santa is your parents?" And I was like, "Ha ha, yes, that is a thing I definitely do know and have known and am not learning right now." I immediately remembered the list I'd emailed Santa the year prior.

I'm sure when I found out that Santa was my parents and that my literal dad had likely received my desperate and horny wish list, I panicked.

I'm sure I paced around my childhood bedroom, coming up with lies to tell my parents when they inevitably confronted me about my crushes. "Actually," I probably practiced to myself in the mirror, "the words 'Matt and Bobby' are code for 'toys,' and 'like me back' is code for 'be my Christmas present.'"

This email to Santa and the revelation of Santa not existing was the exact combination of my personal childhood hell: someone knows your secret and also you don't know a thing that apparently everyone else knows. Yet the idea of my parents finding out who I liked a year earlier was still more cause for immediate concern for me than the fact they had lied about Santa for my entire childhood.

My parents never brought up the email. So, a couple years ago, I asked Mom and Dad if they remembered that twenty-year-old letter I sent to Santa's in-box. Specifically, whether they remembered their reaction when they saw I'd asked for "two boyfriends, please, thanks." To my surprise (and admitted relief), they said they didn't remember it at all and that they were pretty sure they weren't the ones who'd responded. So, unfortunately, twenty-nine-year-old me ended up outing my eight-year-old self to my parents. Also, belated apologies to whichever adult in 1998 read an email to Santa, expecting a wish for a bicycle or book, and got a request from an eight-year-old girl asking for requited love.

I wonder who I would have been in third grade had I not been so concerned with various Matts or Bobbys or Santa. I've spent most of my adulthood unlearning the habit of living solely in relation to the men around me, of developing certain likes or interests or entirely new personalities in hopes that I will be appealing to whoever's male gaze I hoped to attract. Sometimes I wish I could whisper to eight-year-old me the secret it's taken me too long to learn: you get to be a whole entire person independent from who does or does not like you. But I think eight-year-old me needed to learn these things on her own. Also, if I Looper-ed myself back in time to tell this to child-Mia, she definitely would have been more concerned with the fact that *cue panic crying* someone knew about her secret crushes than, oh, I don't know, the fact she was meeting her adult self.

I'm less wary about sharing my own "secrets" than I was when I was younger. (As evidenced by the entirety of this book.) I will gladly divulge my crushes to anyone at any point in time, in part because I am married and my crush, at any given time, is either my husband or the cartoon version of Aladdin. I'm starting to wonder whether that comfort comes from the assumption that everyone else is as concerned with feeling as out of the loop as I am. That I assume I am assuaging someone else's fear of not knowing something.

Vulnerability is still scary to me. It still means the possibility of rejection. It still means the possibility of looking stupid or being embarrassed, arguably the things that scare me most. If Future Me wants to come Looper some advice on overcoming that, it'd be greatly appreciated.

Like Santa predicted, Matt and Bobby never liked me back. I only think about that when I fall back into the hard-to-break habit of trying to remember every crush I've ever had. Based on how accurately I can still recite that list, it was their loss, clearly. That Christmas in 1998, instead of two boyfriends, I got a Furby. In a sense, Santa did get me the requited attention I craved. It just needed batteries.

MANDATORY FUN

Today is my birthday! Let's give a huge congratulations to me on continuing to age, a brave and unique choice. In celebration, I'm thinking that for my birthday we light a dessert on fire. I found this adorable local bakery that will stick a candelabra into the middle of an impossibly small doughnut, which will be perfect. I'm also thinking we should sing a song while the dessert is ablaze. No, the song's not for me—it's for the doughnut. Something like, "Thank you, thank you, doughnut / for letting us put this fire on you" or Britney Spears's version of "My Prerogative."

My favorite part about it being my birthday is how good I am at being the age I am. Everyone looks to me and goes, "Wow! You're already turning *this* age? I thought you were much younger!" This is a compliment to my youthful glow. They also say, "I thought you turned this age long, long ago," which is a compliment to my natural ability for being the age I am. It has nothing to do with my deepening crow's-feet, growing number of gray hairs, the little tummy paunch of old fat that just appears when you turn a certain age, my creaky voice, or the fact that I often break into a cold sweat when I realize that the year 2000 was not ten years ago. I enjoy being my current age and don't panic about it ever!

Unfortunately, I regret to say that I will stop being my current age after a year passes. I know, I'm sad about it too! However, it's important to know when you've overstayed your welcome and, for me, my age can only last one year.

This seems like the perfect opportunity for everyone to go around and say what they're grateful for in regard to me, specifically. Feel free to mention my hair, my outfit, the fact that I stopped wearing that perfume called "Slutty Funnel Cake." There are so many things you have to be grateful for! C'mon, don't be shy. Anyone? All right, well . . . we could do that thing where you all tell me something you wish you would have known when you turned the age I'm turning? You, all, are older than me, right? You had to check a box on the invitation.

Okay, back to the celebration! Making a birthday wish list isn't something people typically do beyond their youth, but you know what they say about age: it's only a number and even crusty dinosaur people like presents. Besides, how else are you supposed to know what to get me? Were you just going to stick a bow on a gift card and hope for the best? Were you . . . not going to get me a gift? Or worse, get me *just* a card and nothing else?!? A card is not a gift; it is a moral conundrum. It says, "Here's this piece of paper to which I've assigned emotional value. Now you have to decide how long you should hold on to it before inevitably tossing it in the recycling bin. Sure hope greeting card glitter is recyclable. Anyway, here's to another year of you being you or whatever!"

By the way, I will be cashing in the "and many more!" part of my birthday well-wishes by continuing to celebrate well past my actual birth date. I deserve a birth week—a birth month, even—for merely existing on this hellscape of a planet. After all, you're only this age once, every day, for an entire year!

On a serious note, I'm so grateful to be surrounded by friends and family as I mark another trip around the sun. It's a privilege, a badge of honor even. However, if I find out anyone with any modicum of success is younger than me, I will fucking murder them. Happy birthday to me!

SHE'S FRIENDLY

My dog, Ava, is an adorable little freak. Just like her mommy. Yes, I call myself "Mommy." It started as a joke when Riley and I first got Ava. We were like, "Ha ha, wouldn't it be funny if we called each other 'Mommy' and 'Daddy,' he-he that'd be so funny." Five years later, I have often said the phrase, "Ava, please stop humping Papa's leg."

I don't know if Ava is a good dog, but she is perfect. I give her kisses on the head every time she makes peepee outside. I feed her all the snacks so she loves me but doesn't respect me. I let her sleep in our bed because it makes me feel big and powerful to know I can take away that privilege at any time. I've yelled at a stray cat to "stay away from my baby," and after we got her, my body instinctively started lactating.

We don't like to say that we rescued Ava because we didn't. She quite literally ran away to our house twice. That sounds like the premise for a dog food commercial or a movie with Christian undertones but all that really means is our house was a straight and direct path from her old house. Her first owner lived one street over from us, no more than a few hundred feet away. I'm assuming Ava, when left outside for more than four seconds, would squoosh her little body between the fence posts, cross the road, trot through neighbors' yards, cross a second road, and only stopped because our front porch was in her path.

The second time Ava showed up at our doorstep—barking like "HELLO I AM BACK ONCE AGAIN DO YOU STILL HAVE . . . I THINK YOU CALLED IT PEANUT BUTTER?"—she ended up staying for good. When Ava's original owner came to pick her up that second time, she was like, "Oh, Ava gets out a lot." And I was like, "Yeah same, me too." And her owner was like, "No, like she runs away a lot." And I was like, "Yeah, same, I run from my feelings too." And she was like, "You can keep her if you want. She seems to like you, and we don't really have as much time for her as she needs." And I was like, "Yes, cool, the dependence is already mutual." Now, I carry around a dog in an elite baby carrier (the front of my hoodie) while drinking white wine. My transition to suburban mom has been swift and effortless.

That's the nice way to explain how we got Ava. There is a different version of the story where we took a puppy from a five-year-old in recovery from leukemia. Let me start by saying everyone is fine and well! Stop worrying! It's fine! Everyone is fine!

Our neighbor, a single parent of two, got Ava for her daughter, who'd been sick, to keep her company. The family needed to leave the house more than expected and Ava is absolutely not a trained service dog, so she was often at home alone. "Alone" is among Ava's least favorite ways to be, second only to "bathed."

They tried to give her to a relative, but Ava refused to eat—Gandhi who?—and she was returned back to our neighbors. So, when Ava "ran away" to our house, her owner seemed both sad and relieved that she'd found a new home for herself. When she came to drop off Ava's kennel, food dish, and a few accessories including a dog-size wedding veil, her two kids came to say goodbye as well. The older of the two asked if they were "really giving her away again." Their mom said yes, and the kids seemed sad and a little dubious but also like they understood in a way I wouldn't imagine my five-year-old self to have understood. If they had changed their minds and taken her home, I would have cried endlessly for this dog I'd known for an afternoon.

The family came to visit Ava once before they eventually moved from the house a street over. Sometimes when we walk past that old house, I stop to see if Ava will stop or sniff around or sigh wistfully. She doesn't because she either has no scent memory of the place or is a stone-cold bitch.

A few fun facts about Ava: she's a mix between a Havanese* and a cotton ball with legs, she loves naps, and she's obsessed with me. My maternal instincts have been fully engaged since we got her. Or whatever instinct it is that makes you want to exploit the things you love for money and internet fame.

If you're hiring, here's a brief rundown of Ava's work experience and special skills. You can contact her assistant (me) for her full résumé, which is an eighteen-minute video of her eating grass.

Strengths:

- Great comedic timing. We have this running bit where she props herself up next to me and emits the squeakiest fart she can.
- Being soft.
- Getting poop caught in her butt fur.
- Rolling on stink bugs (alive or dead).
- Being dependent on me for everything and not chipping in for rent, groceries, Hulu, the little rice crackers I buy for

---

* It's believed that the vast majority of Havanese dogs in the US were bred from eleven dogs brought to the country during the Cuban Revolution in the 1950s. Ava is an inbred little Marxist.

myself and sneak-feed her when Riley isn't paying attention, etc.

- Making her mouth and butthole smell exactly the same.

Weaknesses:

- She barks at the mail carrier, which is very cliché and embarrassing. We'll have to discuss how this is bad for both
our brands. There's a chance she does it to be ironic, which
further proves her excellent grasp of comedy.
- She sheds significantly less than me. Like, at least try to
keep up.
- No thumbs.
- She's probably a Carrie.

Previous Experience:

- Once, I asked Ava to go get her toy, referring to a $1 pur-
ple rope she chews on when she wants to pretend she's a
dog. Knowing that would have been too obvious a choice,
she instead chose to hop on the bed and present me with
a dead spider she found in the corner of the room. This is
the kind of thought leadership Ava consistently brings to
the table. She often makes me ask the big questions like,
"Is my dog funnier than me?"

I never imagined myself with a small dog. I grew up with labs
and collie mixes and just assumed, if I got a dog, it'd be a big, beefy
mountain dog that'd scare off house burglars and let me ride around
on its back. Riley never imagined himself with a dog at all. He still
doesn't, to be fair, and that's fine because Ava is only barely a dog.
She's more like a cat-bunny or a throw pillow you need to feed.

Ava isn't necessarily well-behaved, but she is small. When she does bad things, they too are small. She used to do a tiny protest poop whenever we left the house without her. We'd come home to our bathroom mat adorned with what looked like a single chocolate chip as if to say, *You have inconvenienced me, and I shall do the same.* Eventually, she stopped doing this for the same reason she started: she wanted to and felt like it. She absolutely peed on our new carpet within weeks of its installation, but the way she sad-walked to her kennel—head down, sauntering in sorrow—completely erased any frustration from my brain. When I picked her up to, I guess, apologize, I'm sure she turned to the studio audience and winked.

One of the things Ava does best is sleep. There are so many ways she can sleep: belly up, splayed legs, tucked snout, pillow sandwich, leg-pit snuggle, lap lay, donut. For donut, she curls tightly into her own body, making herself so small that if I think about it too hard, I will cry. I ask her questions about her process ("Are you so small? Are you so tiny and small?") but she refuses to answer. I respect her for keeping some things private.

Ava dreams. Or does things that make it seem like she dreams. My favorite is this one we call "sleep bubbles," where she barks while asleep. It sounds like she's going GRRROOOOOOWLYIP while underwater. If my iCloud ever gets hacked and its contents leaked, the world will be blessed with three thousand hours of me recording Ava's sleep bubbles and a bunch of screenshots I took by accident. Ava also runs in her sleep, paddling her tiny paws ever so slightly. This is only worth noting because she does not run in real life. She loves the idea of a walk much more than the act of walking.

I imagine that, when Ava dreams, she is imagining one of two things: chasing deer or finding acorns. The girl would run away with a family of deer if I'd let her or if she were just a tiny bit faster. The handful of times she's gotten close enough to the deer before they ran away, she was gleeful. She got closer to them than she will most other dogs. I fear that she would run away with most forest creatures if she met them. She's gotten far too close to raccoons and possums for my comfort. She's like Snow White but a dog and tone-deaf.

Ava's favorite treat, aside from every sun-dried worm she finds, is acorns. She loves to do this form of performance art where she presents me with some old, gross nut she found outside. This becomes a game where I will take the nut from her and throw it back outside. Then, when she goes outside, she'll retrieve the same nut or perhaps a different nut and bring it back in the house. Sometimes I won't catch her until I hear her crunching. Then, I have to be like, "What you eating?!" and I swear she starts crunching faster. It'd be annoying if she wasn't so cute.

It's impossible to talk about your dog in a way that isn't stupid. When we thought Ava might have a UTI, Riley and I had to figure out how to say, "It looks like she has some irritation on her . . . peepee." We have since learned, through correction by a vet, that the proper word to use is *vulva* as in "She might need to wear a cone to keep her from licking her vulva." It should be illegal to say your dog has a vagina.

Should you ever need to talk about a dog's anatomy, allow me to impart the ways I've described Ava's little dunkaroo of a body unto you:

- I used phrases like "dunkaroo," which connote zero meaning whatsoever. It's meant to evoke her overall aesthetic and I've found sounds and nonsense words are more effective than anatomical ones. I feel like you understand exactly what I mean when I say Ava walks in a way that goes "dink-donk."
- Her hind legs are exclusively referred to as her "two chickens in the back."

- Her nipples are located on her "peepee tummy."
- Her chest is where she keeps all her brave.
- Her nose is a snoot and her tiny lips are where she is the most baby.
- When she makes her legs completely limp, they become her jelly.
- Ava has "tiny corn teeth," meaning her teeth are the exact proportions of an ear of baby corn.

I think a lot about what Ava will be like if/when Riley and I have kid(s). Will she hate them? Love them? Avoid them? Be obsessed with them? Will she lick their head like a mama dog with her puppies? Will she lick their head the way she licks the space between my fingers: obsessively and with a kind of fervor that makes me wonder what disgusting thing she is tasting? What will she be like if I ever get pregnant? Will she rest her snoot on my growing belly? Will she bark if she feels the baby kick? Will she find a way to nestle into my pregnancy pillows? Will I buy her pregnancy pillows of her own? How many pregnancy pillows is too many to buy for your spayed dog?

Ava is pretty good around kids. She is a creature that loves attention, and children who are excited to meet a dog want nothing more than to give that dog all the attention their tiny bodies can muster. It helps that Ava is the exact right size for a toddler. She's not too tall or too little. She's sturdy enough not to get tumbled around by a kid but not so big she'll knock them down. She feels the right amount of soft, has ears with just enough flop, a tail with the right kind of wag. Seeing Ava happily trot away as my nieces gleefully chase after her is the definition of precious. It's so sweet it hurts but you can't look away. The most adorable kind of masochism.

Ava's good about not jumping up on kids, which has absolutely nothing to do with training on my and Riley's part. We've taught her nothing aside from what "treat" means and how to get what you want through guilt and being cute. She knows that the words *do you want* come before words like *yummy treat, walk, car,* or *outside* and will stomp her little paws in anticipation, like, "Hell yeah, I want."

When we tried to teach her how to sit, she refused. She ended up just lying down. So we pretended we were actually trying to teach her how to lie down the entire time. Then, one day, she decided she wanted to sit. Of course, not how most dogs sit; Ava loves to keep you on your toes. Now, when Ava hears the command "sit," she sits on her haunches, balancing only on her two back legs. She brings her paws up to her chest and her little pink belly makes an itty-bitty paunch. She looks like a dog doing a good impression of a prairie dog, or maybe the other way around. When she's feeling extrashowy, she sticks her tongue out the tiniest bit.

When my sister, Ana, stayed with us during the pandemic, she was determined to teach Ava "shake." Riley and I were like, "good luck" and offered only emotional support. To our surprise, Ava quickly picked up the new trick. Now, when you say "paw" she gives you one or both of her paws like an orphan child begging, "Please, sir, a crumb?" Ava also learned an entirely different trick called, "Hand-Feed Me My Dinner, Why Don't You?"

When Ana came home from work at night, she'd play with Ava for a while, usually using her food as little treats. Sometimes Ana would just let Ava have a couple bits of kibble out of her hand, because sometimes it's fun to play Petting Zoo with your own dog. Unfortunately, Ava then associated Ana coming home with dinner-time and, for weeks, would only eat food if Ana fed it to her, a few pieces at a time, by hand. She's back to her normal eating schedule now: ignoring her food that is available to her the entire day, getting "hungry" when we're at our friends' house and they're feeding their normal dog who eats normal meals, pouting that she doesn't get to eat Other Dinner, coming home and eventually eating her actual food at 1:00 a.m., loudly crunching as we're trying to fall asleep. Afterward, she comes and put her paws up on my side of the bed, like, "I am ready to retire to my sleep spot now." I pick her up and she pretends to help by making a little "humph" noise when I lift her. She burps in my face and licks her ass until she eventually falls asleep.

It's only fair I tell you the worst thing about Ava, who is otherwise obviously perfect. She barks so, so much. Well, not *so* much but enough that people know she barks. Like I mentioned before, she barks at the mail carrier. She also barks when someone is at the door. She barks when she *thinks* someone is at the door, but it was just a particularly loud gust of wind. She barks when she thinks someone is coming toward our house. She barks when she hears a car door shut outside because, holy shit, they might be coming toward our house! Once, I caught Ava staring at herself in the mirror while she barked, something that just further affirms my suspicion that she is a human reincarnated as this small loaf of a dog. Ava also has a bad habit of barking at people who don't pay attention to her, children included. I've tried explaining to her many times that what she is doing is counterproductive. You cannot yell "HEY, GET OVER HERE, I LOVE YOU" to a complete stranger and expect them to actually approach. Ava still hasn't grasped this concept and I don't know if she ever will. Maybe I should give her some literature on the subject?

Ava barks at passersby if she can see them out the window. Again, it seems less protective and more performative. Like, *Woof woof, I'll play your little game where I do dog things like "paw" and "walk," but just know, this is also what comes with the territory.* Ava barks when she hears the sound of another dog walking by. Yes, really. She hears the sound of the dog's collar or leash and feels the need to scream out the window about it. If she were to actually meet any of the dogs she barks at, she'd cower behind my legs, pushing her face into my calf hoping that if she can't see them, the inverse might be true. Ava likes the other dogs more in theory than in practice. She isn't really a dog person.

Sometimes I ask Ava if she wants a puppy, like how you'd ask a child if they want a puppy. "Should Mommy get you a puppy?" She'd love the puppy until it got too big and then she'd look at it, like, "Who the fuck parked this semitruck in the house?" I think Ava would do well with a little bird. One that could say, "How are you doin'?" in a robotic but eerily human way. I think they'd pay attention to each other equally as little, which is exactly what Ava looks for in any nonhuman companion. Also, sometimes Ava looks like a cockatoo and I'd love to introduce her to an actual cockatoo so she'd finally get the reference. Unfortunately, Ava would ultimately have a terribly imbalanced relationship with any pet/ward, one that would cause years of therapy down the road. Ava believes she is the center of all life in the universe, and she is correct in that assumption.

Not to be dramatic, but if she ever dies, I'll kill her.

SHY: F.A.Q.

What does *Shy* mean?

Shy refers to being reserved, specifically in the company of others. Shyness is usually associated with quietness, timidity, and holding your bladder for too long because it might be rude to get up and pee. Shy can also mean "less than"—e.g., *She was an inch shy of being considered "so tall it's loud."*—which is a little on the nose but that's fine, I guess.

How do you know if you're Shy?

The fact that you asked means you aren't Shy. Shy people don't ask questions. They sit quietly in the back of the class and mentally will their questions to be answered by the teacher or they just google it later.

Is it the same as being an introvert?

Not always. You can absolutely be a boisterous introvert—this is also referred to as being a "method actor." If you've heard someone profess "I am an introvert," that may be true but they are not Shy. Shy people do not profess.

If someone is being Shy, does that mean they don't like me?

Probably. You seem like someone who needs to be reminded that it's okay if people don't like you.

That's presumptuous but true. Are Shy people smart?

Shy people are too Shy to talk about their intellect, which, in turn, makes them smart.

What do Shy people eat?

Soft breads, cooked carrots, basically anything that doesn't create a loud crunch or draw attention to itself by requiring silverware. Shy people are allowed one (1) bag of Doritos per year, but it must be opened in the bathroom and they must cough when they do so.

Where do Shy people live?

Cheyenne, Wyoming. Not because the first syllable sounds like "shy" but because it is an unassuming place, and no one knows anything about it.

What do Shy people do for work?

Anything that doesn't require talking on the phone or saying the phrase, "Could I have everyone's attention?"

What are some hobbies that Shy people have?

Petting dogs at parties, hiding in hoodies, and practicing saying "uh, someone's in here" in the bathroom.

Are Shy people allowed to use caps lock?

No. To type in a normal-size font is even too outgoing. Shy people prefer to type in a subscript or, at the very most, a 6-point font. Never bold. Often italicized. Italics are the whisper of fonts.

What do Shy people sound like?

Kind of like "Um, hi, I was just wondering if you were saving this chair for someone." Or a gentle breeze.

Do Shy people ever yell?

Every Shy person is allotted three (3) screams throughout their lifetime. These must be done at the bottom of the ocean or in outer space. All astronauts are Shy, which is why they chose a profession that allows them to be as far away from other people as humanly possible. Also, no one can hear it when they fart.

Can Shy people love?

Yes, but they do so coyly. Shy people express love by holding their hands behind their back and looking up in a "who me?" Minnie Mouse–esque way.

Are there any famous Shy people?

Not currently. All famous Shy people are dead. In fact, a famous person can only become Shy when they die. Being dead is the most quiet way to live.

PART 5

Mind Your Manners

MIDWEST NICE

"Ope" is among the most well-known midwestern niceties. It can mean everything from "you made a mistake" to "I made a mistake—sorry there, bud" to "gall-dangit, I thought this Farm & Fleet coupon was still valid."

Like the Bible Belt, the culture of the Midwest is deeply intertwined with Christianity. Many will attend First Communion parties as often as they will birthday parties. Practicing Catholics may take part in the sacrament of reconciliation, which is the one where you confess you're "just gonna sneak by ya" as you enter the church pew. Some will receive the sacrament of atonement: the apologetic eye contact you make as you shuffle sideways to your seat, your crotch to your pew-mate's face in a God-honoring way.

"Jesus, Mary, and Joseph" may sound religious, but it is as close to an expletive as your grandma will ever say.

If you are visiting the Midwest, there are a few courtesies you'll want to adopt, the foremost of which is Feigned Familiarity. When passing another car in your neighborhood, it is required you look the other driver in the eye and raise your hand slightly from the steering wheel as you drive by. Similarly, when you cross another person on the sidewalk, it's customary to nod and smile very slightly at each other as if to say, *Yes, hello. We are both humans existing in the same space.* This is sometimes accompanied by a "hi" so quiet and breathy it's imperceptible to nonmidwestern ears.

For those in Wisconsin, Minnesota, Michigan, and parts of Illinois, when someone asks about your weekend plans, a brief and acceptable answer is "goin' Up North." No need to go into any further detail lest you waste their time and make them miss the Packers' kickoff. "Goin' Up North" is shorthand for, "I'm going to my grandma's house on Lake Winnebago. I will likely fish, barf off the side of a boat while my cousins go tubing, or, if I'm lucky, both."

The words *yeah* and *no* can be repeated and combined in an infinite number of ways to convey a wide range of human emotion. "Yeah, no" means "You are correct in assuming the answer is no." "No, yeah" means "Don't second-guess yourself. The answer is yes." "Yeah, no, yeah" loosely translates to "Of course" or "Obviously" or "It's no biggie, hon." Its antonym is "No, yeah, no," which means "No way" or "Not a chance" or "I'm not going into Piggly Wiggly the Wednesday before Thanksgiving, are you nuts?" "No no no" means the Packers fumbled the dang ball again. "Yeah yeah yeah" is what I say when I'm lying about being able to drive confidently in the snow.

The northern Midwest accent is, arguably, the nicest accent. Not aurally. God, no. It's nasal and loud, like trumpet with a sinus infection. However, the northern Midwest accent (think: Fargo, Upper Michigan, all of Minnesota, the voice you make when you say "dontcha know") is a kind accent. It's one that disarms and invites you in for supper. It sounds like a warm hug, like Santa's smile, like someone offering you a cold beer because they probably are literally offering you a cold beer. In terms of kind accents, it's second only to Canada.

There are only three reasons one can leave someone's house in the Midwest: (1) you need to beat the weather; (2) you need to go check on your slow cooker; (3) the house is on fire.

To be a true Midwesterner, you must perfect the Midwestern

Goodbye. While an Irish Goodbye involves sneaking out unnoticed, the Midwestern Goodbye is a ritual that takes at least an hour, making known your gratitude for being in attendance and your sorrow in needing to depart. Get familiar with phrases like "Make sure you tell Barb I say hi" and "Don't forget to grab some leftovers to take home," which is how you bid guests farewell. Midwesterners have been passing the same stained Tupperware container back and forth for generations.

Regardless of the weather, it's common courtesy to forget a mitten wherever you go. In that sense, a Midwesterner never truly leaves.

IF YOU NEED ANYTHING, MY NAME IS MIA

Welcome! I'm so glad you're here. If you need any-thing, my name is Mia. Really, don't hesitate to ask. I'll just be right over here.

Just so you know, we are running a sale right now: anything with a blue tag is buy one, get one half off. Anything with a red tag is buy one, get one free. Anything with an orange tag is something I, per-sonally, don't recommend you buy on account of it being ugly. Any-thing with a purple tag is from my own wardrobe, and I just want to get a second opinion on it. If you see what looks like a brown tag, I wouldn't touch that if I were you. Same with a white tag. If you hap-pen to find a tag with a smiley face, let me know—a customer mis-placed some LSD while trying things on and won't stop hounding me about where it is. Anything with a green tag can be shoplifted, and I'll just look the other way. If you see a yellow tag, that's actually a mustard stain and, again, you can just grab that and go. We've got mustard packets at the front if you need extra. Everything else is complimentary with a $10,000 purchase.

Can I get you something to drink? Just a water for now? Would you like sparkling or still? That's where I either come back with a

LaCroix and a mouthful of sparklers or I remain motionless while spitting tap water out of my mouth like a fountain. A Coke? I'm so sorry. I hate to be the person to say this, but is Pepsi okay? It's not? Okay. No, it's fine, I've just never had anyone say that it wasn't okay. No, no, I'll get you a Coke. It's no trouble at all. Yeah, I can get it for you. I know a girl who can be here in, like, ten, fifteen minutes max. Yeah, yeah, she's good for it. She's gotten me some before, she's cool. You're fine to hang for a bit? Awesome, I'll get you those sparklers while we wait.

Yes, we've also got food here. Super yummy! If you're interested, our soup of the day is tomato basil bisque, our happy hour ends whenever you say it does, and today's specials include seasonal hometown nostalgia, me flirting with you a little bit, and a gorgeous pan-fried salmon with a ginger-soy reduction.

Again, if you need anything, I'm Mia. If you don't need anything, I'll still be Mia but sadder.

Have you been in before? Excellent. Well, we do things family-style here. That means that whatever you buy, you have the option to ask me to come and look at it disapprovingly. I can also say things like, "Wow! Looks great!" or "Wait, is that my top? What the fuck, Beth? I told you I've been looking for that." Oh, and everything comes with a coupon for one (1) holiday where I'll come home with you and tell your parents we're dating.

Do you want me to start a room for you? Not yet? Do you want a shopping cart? A basket? I could walk a couple steps behind you and quietly hold your purse? Act like a sentient coatrack? A coat closet with legs and average-size boobs? No, really it's no trouble!

Oh, speaking of basket, do you need me to refill your bread-basket? Yep, it doubles as a breadbasket. We've got white, wheat, sourdough, rye, marbled rye, rhino-shaped, some Wonder Bread I packed down into a dense ball, a loaf of bread I stole to feed my sister's children, a loaf of bread I stole with my pet monkey Abu, a loaf of bread I can multiply to feed thousands, and pumpernickel.

Want me to start a tab for you? You sure? I can use my card? Okay, well, let me know if you change your mind.

Need any help finding something? I'm more than happy to help.

A little story about me. Every personality test I have ever taken has deemed me a "helper" by nature. Aside from one time, in high school, when we took a survey to see what jobs we'd be best suited for; my top result was "clown." Can you believe that? Otherwise, it usually came up with stuff like hospitality worker, nurse, teacher, day care provider, babysitter you accidentally call "Mom," the person in the friend group who keeps offering water and ibuprofen, and actual mom.

Ha ha, okay, I'll give you a minute. Holler if you need anything!

You doing all right? Great. Again, my name is Mia, but it's okay if you accidentally call me Mya or Nia or Mom.

Are you looking for anything specific? Anything vague? Just looking? Great, well, we've actually got another deal going where if you stare at anything for too long, I'll see if you want me to buy it for you like Daddy Warbucks. I'll even shave my head. Perfect, just let me know. I'll be around if you need me.

All right, here's that three-layered cake, and I'll be back with your fifteen-foot cheese platter in just a bit. Yeah, actually, the guy over there bought them for you, but I can send them back if you'd prefer. Totally understand if it's weird. If you want, I can tell him we're together so he backs off a bit. No problem at all! Let me know if you change your mind.

Can I get anything else for you? More napkins? Extra plates? A kidney? Two kidneys? Three? Our chef has excellent kidneys.

All set? Do you know our return policy? Anything you purchase can be exchanged for store credit with a receipt. If you don't have a receipt, I'll still give you store credit, you just have to say "please" and tear up a little bit. If you want cash, that's fine, you'll just have to rob us. I can get you the key to the safe, but you have to promise you'll give it back. Yeah, take whatever you want from there, but if the key goes missing, my boss will kill me.

Save any room for dessert? Yeah, I know, just wanted to be polite. Just the check then? All together? Split two ways, between me and you? You split and I take it out of my paycheck? We both get the hell out of here and just see what happens?

Oh, you're leaving? Did you find everything you were looking for today? You can tell me if you didn't. Well, I want to know if you needed something I couldn't give to you. Because maybe I could— we've got stock in the back. No? Okay, well, you know how you can reach me if you ever change your mind.

Thanks for coming in! Come back soon! I love you!

TO HELL AND BACK

The times I've felt most certain there is a God are when I thought that he was mad at me. Church was for staring at other people's families and getting glimpses of Father Steve's sneakers, trying to picture this man of God at a Payless. (Like teachers and gynecologists, priests evaporate if they leave their place of work.) Communion was for seeing how long I could keep the host—body of Christ if you're nasty/Catholic—in my mouth before it disintegrated into Styrofoam goop. Praying had a dual purpose: keeping the Bad Nighttime Thoughts at bay and a preemptive measure of protection just in case a murderer or ghost child came to get me. The Our Father is a magic spell you say to make yourself unhauntable. A couple Hail Marys and any serial killer will skip your room on their murderous rampage. (At least, if your family gets murdered, it'll give Brian G. a reason to talk to you in biology!) Sunday school was for being intimidated by and desperately seeking the approval of the instructor who was also my classmate's mom, Patricia. As a parent, teacher, and religious conduit, Ms. Patricia was my personal holy trinity.

God was there when I least expected it but not to provide any sense of solace or hope. When I closed a door to go to seedy chat rooms in middle school, God peered in through an opened window like a holy firewall. (No cybering until marriage!) God was there when I discovered that the Oxygen network plays soft-core porn after midnight. He was there when I stuffed my bra with balled-up socks and marveled at my new pair of hard, lumpy boobs in the bathroom mirror. He'd show up immediately after I rubbed my crotch against the arm of the sofa—classic God. He'd be there if I spent too much time wondering what other household objects I could rub my crotch with, usually popping in to be like, "I see you ogling the soapy shower washcloth. You know your dad washes his ass with that?"

Divine intervention didn't come when I prayed school would get canceled so I wouldn't have to give my social studies presentation. I didn't feel particularly Saved when I came back from my church's weeklong mission retreat where I painted houses and developed unrequited crushes on young Christians from around the country. God did not work in mysterious ways. He was extremely on the nose and always popped up when I was about to do a really good sin.

In that sense, it's only natural I spent much of fifth grade convinced I was going to hell. My mortal sin occurred in an educational toy store called Zany Brainy. Just as the scripture predicted.

I was there with my mom and three siblings, probably shopping for discounted computer games or off-brand Silly Putty. Because I was ten and because the store was only about as big as an elementary school cafeteria, I was allowed to roam around alone. This worked out well as I was already experimenting with the feeling of complete humiliation whenever I was anywhere in public with my family. For context, this was around the same time I exclusively wore my hair in tight ponytails with two thin, greasy strips of hair out in the front, framing my face in a way that wasn't flattering but at least took me a long time to do. Embarrassment is relative.

Left to my own devices and bad taste, I went straight to the section of the store that sold Cool Things for Tween Girls. These things mostly included beads to make necklaces, beads to make bracelets, beads to make key chains, beads to make art, beads for your hair and body and emotional well-being, and clear boxes in which to store, stare at, and think about your beads. If there's one thing stores think girls love, it's beads. And you know what? They're right. I remember exactly how a clear plastic bag of pony beads smells, and you're right to assume that, on at least one occasion, I've stared at an array of those gorgeous, shiny little plastic nuggets and thought, *I'm gonna eat that.*

My Zany Brainy sin was not eating the plastic beads. I have too great a fear of choking in public and am even more afraid of the idea of bothering someone to do the Heimlich on me. It's actually very noble to suffocate to death because you didn't want to be rude and interrupt someone else's day.

Whilst perusing the Cool Things for Tween Girls, I saw a "tattoo" kit that contained a small plastic bucket (how kitsch!) and paper stencils shaped like hearts and lightning bolts (how edgy!). It also had a set of small shitty markers that often come included in bad craft sets, oddly colored and somehow already dried out. It was less "tattoo kit" and more "draw on yourself with markers to feel something." I obviously needed it.

I knew it was wrong to use something that didn't belong to me, especially if that something was still in store packaging. Unlike the display shoes at Kohl's or the plastic tray piled with room-temperature cheese at Piggly Wiggly, I knew the tattoo kit at the front of the shelf was not for sampling. I knew I wasn't supposed to remove the marker from the pack and take it for a test spin, and I knew this would make trying it out feel even better.

After what I'm assuming was an extremely conspicuous glance from left to right, I snuck the small light blue marker out of the top of the kit and slid it up my hoodie sleeve. I had no intent to take this stolen souvenir home with me; I really did just want to try it out. What made *this* marker a tattoo marker? It didn't look different from any other RoseArt-variety marker but maybe that was the point? Maybe it was supposed to look washable when, in fact, it was actually a Sharpie in disguise. Maybe "semipermanent" was code for "stains your skin for life"? Maybe it would hurt like a real tattoo?! I had to find out.

With the contraband up my sleeve, I tiptoed—probably literally, again I'm sure I was extremely suspicious—to a back corner of the store. I, a ten-year-old, pretended to peruse a baby book display. After fiddling with a board book for a few seconds or maybe forty-five minutes, I let the marker gently fall out of my sleeve into my hand. It's a maneuver I've since only used for similar contraband: slipping a tampon to a friend or jostling out the weed pen I snuck into the bathroom of an off-brand Cirque du Soleil show.

I uncapped the tattoo marker and pressed the felt tip to my skin. The rush! The thrill! The pressure to think of something to draw! I settled on a tiny blue heart on my wrist—I know the '90s kids are shaking with nostalgia. The result was hard to see due to my poor art skills and the pen being, as I'd feared, a literal craft store marker. My first tattoo was perfect.

I marveled at my new ink for a moment, satisfied that it looked okay but not so good I'd need to convince my mom to buy me the whole kit. I pulled a reverse marker-down-the-sleeve maneuver and started walking back to the Cool Things for Tween Girls display to put the pen back in its case. But there, standing next to the tattoo kit was the devil himself: a Zany Brainy employee with spiky bleached hair, arms crossed over his blue work vest. Satan is real and he frosts his tips.

"Do you know where this pen went?" he asked, gesturing to the tattoo kit sitting at the front of the shelf. *With me to hell*, I thought. In my memory, the employee is both without age and exactly twenty-five years old. He seems mean but doesn't yell, which is among the scariest ways to be mean. He doesn't seem mad . . . maybe just a little smug? Happy even? Like, catching me doing a Bad Thing is a perk of the job. In hindsight, I'm sure he was just annoyed and didn't really give a shit about the marker.

"No," I answered quietly while trying not to cry. Is there anything more embarrassing than being greeted by the literal devil and *crying*? He definitely didn't believe me but walked away regardless. The moment he turned his back, I let the marker fall out of my sleeve onto the store's carpeted floor and ran-walked back to my mom. I told her the employee was "acting weird to me," omitting the part about the tattoo marker. She shrugged it off, and we left soon after. I had escaped the first circle of hell.

Then came the plagues of stomach-wrenching guilt and nightmares where I was lost in a department store, stuck sifting through human-size Tupperware containers of nothing for eternity. Often, after a bad thing happened or a good thing didn't happen I'd think, *This is punishment for the Zany Brainy thing*. Sometimes when the phone rang, I'd convince myself it was the mall police arranging a time to come collect me. I wondered what the statute of limitations was on someone thinking you were shoplifting.

Once, months later, I thought I could atone for my almost-sin by getting through a state fair house of mirrors with my brother Zoey. The two of us reached a hallway that looked like it had no floor, and we were both too afraid to move. I wondered whether an act of low-stakes bravery was redeemable for hell credit. I knew the hallway did in fact have a floor but it still felt scary. Similarly, I had no intent to steal the tattoo marker but the employee still thought I did. The exchange rate made sense to me. Ultimately, someone working at the fair ended up shepherding us out the entrance. To my relief and dismay, we never had to cross the hallway.

I don't know if I've ever actually believed in hell as a physical place. As someone who was and maybe always will be motivated by guilt, I absolutely believed my sins—big, small, pseudo, or otherwise—would be punished in some capacity. But even as a fifth grader, the idea of hell as a fiery abyss where you burn eternally seemed . . . kinda campy. Like, what's next: angels have literal wings made of feathers and God is an old white man with a big beard? Grow up.

In my ten-year-old mind, I didn't feel like I needed to transcend the corporeal plane to experience suffering of biblical proportions. Hell was the feeling I got when my classmate heard me fart during a CPR demonstration. (Heaven was another classmate blaming my fart on the first kid.) When my parents spent an afternoon trying to locate my thirteen-year-old whereabouts, hell was the silent car ride home from the Big Lots clearance store. Cell-phone-less and uncontactable, my friend Sami and I had spent literal hours spraying ourselves with $2 perfume and peeing our pants laughing in the laxative aisle. It was the best worst day.

Hell was within walking distance, accessible by a road paved with full-body palpitations of guilt, shame, and humiliation. It was the exact mix of emotions I felt when confronted by the Zany Brainy employee, the same feelings that followed me out the store doors and haunted me to sleep. Hell was waking up in the middle of the night engulfed in my own sweaty fear of being caught despite, arguably, not doing anything worth catching. It was someone, anyone, thinking I'd done a Bad Thing, thus damning me to the eternity of being a Bad Person. In that sense, I spent much of fifth grade living in my own personal hell.

I shoplifted for the first and only time a couple years ago. Obviously, it was from Target and obviously, I took a one-piece swimsuit.

Until I am allowed to sunbathe naked in my backyard without fear that my neighbors will call the cops or dox my titties on the internet, I figure I deserve to do an occasional steal from a big-box retailer like any red-blooded American.

I thought about what I'd do if I got caught shoplifting the swimsuit, how I'd lie in a convincing enough way to not get in trouble. *Oh my gosh! By accident, another much cheaper item must have accidentally gotten caught underneath the one-piece when I scanned it in the self-checkout, and I accidentally didn't pay for the swimsuit by accident! My very accidental mistake!* Had I been caught, I know I only would have felt bad because whoever caught me would've assumed I was the kind of person who steals, which, to be fair, would have been an accurate appraisal of the situation. I couldn't have explained, "No, no, you see, I don't do this kind of thing. I did do it today but I usually don't and so this isn't really me." In my very good and healthy brain, to be thought of as someone who steals is worse than actually stealing.

When I eventually told my mom about the Zany Brainy incident years after it happened, she nodded once and then forgot about it entirely. Unlike my ten-year-old self had imagined, the revelation didn't send her into a shock of fury and disappointment. I don't think she even thought I'd done anything wrong. In my very good and healthy mind, this was as good as being forgiven for my imagined sin.

Whatever lesson I should have learned from the Tattoo Marker Fiasco of 2000 never stuck. I've gotten scolded for trying out nail polish at CVS as a full-blown adult. Any residual guilt I feel about the stolen Target swimsuit dwindles each time I put it on. I don't know if that guilt will ever disappear entirely, but I like how the suit's high cut makes my ass look. It's as close to heaven on earth as I've yet to experience.

Like one might revisit an old boyfriend's Facebook page, I recently googled Zany Brainy. To save you the search, the results don't go too deep.* Their website is mostly defunct and their Instagram bio says the store "was known as 'The World's Greatest Good-for-Kids Toy Store.'" *Was* being the operative word. The retailer filed for bankruptcy and later closed for good in 2001, the same year I graduated from fifth grade. Perhaps the thing with the tattoo marker impacted us equally.

To be honest, while writing this piece, I did have a brief moment of panic about the financial implications of the tattoo marker incident, how the Zany Brainy employee was probably more concerned about his dwindling hours and being let go than me being a sneaky child. In my panic, I wondered whether my ten-year-old choices hurried along the demise of this obsolete educational toy store in some butterfly effect kind of way. And then I remembered I LITERALLY DIDN'T EVEN TAKE THE MARKER.

I had an even briefer moment where I thought about trying to find the employee from the Glendale, Wisconsin, Zany Brainy to . . . I don't know, apologize? Reminisce? Explain myself on the off chance he remembers and still thinks I stole the marker? Even now, I am unable to rid myself of the idea that being thought of as someone who does a bad thing is as hellish, if not worse, than actually doing the bad thing. Hell is other people knowing who I am when I'm alone.

---

* This search also surfaced a community Facebook group called "What Happened to Zany Brainy??" It has 2.1k likes and a post from 2011 that reads, "Zany misses all those that miss it."

MOTHER MAY I?

Mother, may I take one step?

Mother, may I take another step?

Mother, may I take a third step? No, I'm not walking too slow! Yes, I'm wearing the uncomfortable shoes you warned me about, and yes, they're giving me a blister.

Mother, may I take ten tiny steps? He-he. Mother, look how small I'm stepping!

Mother, may I sit down? My feet hurt. Yeah, from the shoes. Okay, but how much longer is it going to be because I'm getting tired already.

Mother, may I walk this way? It's down a dark alley labeled "beware," but I think I should be good. Please, Mother!?

Mother, may I walk *this* way? Do you see how I'm walking? It's like a crab? Do I look like a crab, Mother?

Mother, may I "Walk This Way" by Run-D.M.C. featuring Aerosmith?

Mother, may I take one normal step? It'll be so normal, I promise.

Mother, may I take two steps? Two giant leaps to the right? Left foot, let's stomp?

Mother, may I cha-cha real smooth?

Mother, may I "Cupid Shuffle?"

Mother, may I rent *Step Up 2: The Streets*? No, you don't have to have seen the first one to understand this one, but if you haven't seen it, we should watch it. It has Channing Tatum dancing in water! I don't remember if he does that in *Magic Mike*. We could watch that one next? Actually, forget all that—let's just watch *Magic Mike XXL*.

Mother, may I run really fast for three seconds? Okay, two seconds? Okay, one and a half seconds? How far do you think I can make it in one second? Mother, do you think I'm faster than our neighbor, Trenton?

Mother, may I step away for a bit? I've seen the error in my ways and think it'd be best to give us both some time to process.

Mother, I'm back. Did you miss my stepping?

Step, may I take one mother?

Ha ha, did you hear what I said, Mother? I asked the step if I could take one of you. Did you hear me? Why didn't you laugh then?

Mother, Trenton told me I can take a running jump? What does that mean, Mother? Is it rude?

Mother, may I step on Trenton's ankles?

Mother, may I karate chop the sun? I've been practicing and I think I can finally do it.

Mother, may I try to fly? I bet I could do it this time. What if I only start from the second-highest step?

Mother, may I do three hops like a frog? Ew, Mother, the ground feels crunchy and wet!

Mother, may I get a wet wipe?

Mother, I'm done with the wet wipe now. You can have it back.

Mother, may I move it, move it?

Mother, may I run like the wind, Bullseye?

Mother, may I do the running man? Am I doing it? Is this it?

Mother, may I go outside? Can I come back in? Wait, may I actually go back outside once more? I forgot my Popsicle stick.

Mother, may I take two steps forward, one step back?

Mother, may I start again? I lost count.

Mother, may I take three steps north, two steps southeast, one step west, and four steps south?

Mother, I am lost.

...Mother?

MIND YOUR MANNERS

When I was younger, I used to practice balancing a book on my head. I'd seen it in movies where girls are taught to become women by having good posture and passing tests based on different types of forks. I loved movies like *What a Girl Wants*, *Sydney White*, and *She's the Man*—pretty much anything from Amanda Bynes's oeuvre—where a gawky, out-of-place teen has to fit in with some type of high society group. She starts out a mess, using a napkin the wrong way or wanting to wear sneakers with a ball gown (quirky!). She changes to fit in; this is usually accompanied by a makeover montage and a pop song with lyrics like, "Is this really who I'm meant to be?" Her dramatic change either works or it doesn't, but she ultimately ends up learning that being herself, the way she was at the beginning of the story, is the best way to be. Cue end credits and blooper reels. Of course, none of that stuck with me. All I got was, "Put book on head to be fancy."

I'd find a medium-size book—perhaps a *Chicken Soup for the Soul*—and rest it atop my skull. Sometimes I used paperback books even though I knew that was technically cheating, but who's keeping score, you know? I'd usually end up cocking my head to the side and holding my arms out a little to make the book stay put, like the purpose of the exercise was not to maintain a stick-straight back or keep my chin up but to be the Best Book-Balancing Girl this side of the Mississippi.

You'll be unsurprised to know that I love manner-focused advice columns. Who are these adult people still asking questions of Miss Manners, someone who is a self-described "perfect lady in an imperfect society"? Who is turning to Dear Abby to figure out how to ignore their chatty neighbor in a nice way? More importantly, why is no one paying me a retainer to answer questions about how to deal with shitty extended family or coworkers with no understanding of personal space?

I love advice columns as a concept, especially when people are seeking advice that boils down to, "I mean, you could confront them? You'll seem like an asshole but at least they'll leave you alone." Does anyone actually want advice? Or do we just want third-party validation? Do we seek permission from some unconnected authority figure to act on our desire to set our neighbor's shrubs ablaze, to pour hot coffee on the computer of an inappropriate boss, to disregard all social niceties and just say, "Could you actually . . . stop?" Maybe it's all of the above.

Here, in short, is what most every advice column sounds like:

Dear Mommy,
Someone is doing something I don't like. We have a complex history, and I cannot be honest with them lest it implode our relationship and I, myself, implode with it. They hold some sort of power over me, be it emotional, at work, in our community, or just in my head. Also, they're my mother-in-law! How can I make the bad thing stop without telling them to stop it?
Sincerely,
Your Little Poopy Baby

Dear LPB,
I hear you. All relationships are difficult, and maintaining a bal-
ance of honesty and decorum is tough. Your best option is to say
how you feel and hope for the best. I can't believe you haven't
thought of that on your own!

Best of luck,
Mommy

My family was big on manners. Not the kind with elaborate
table settings or curtsying—though I would have killed to have an
excuse to wear elbow-length gloves. We didn't do "sir" or "ma'am,"
but friends' parents were always Mr. or Mrs. Last Name. Address-
ing an adult by "Lisa" or "Steve" felt like swearing in front of my
parents. *You called them* what*?!* We always said "please" and "thank
you," sometimes like it was a competition. Being the first person to
say "thanks, I love you" after my mom made dinner or our dad gave
us a gift was an unspoken badge of honor. It would cause a waterfall
of "thank yous," each successive sibling echoing the one before. My
parents would say "you're welcome" to each one of us.

My older brother, Zoey, my younger brother, Frankie, my younger
sister, Ana, and I were nothing if not well-behaved. It was something
other adults praised our parents for and, in turn, our parents would
praise us. We were never noisy at church. We tried not to push or
shove or complain too loudly when waiting in any kind of line. We
didn't fight when we went out to dinner. In the car beforehand and
on the ride home after? Ruthlessly and with tears, but the second
the minivan's automatic door started opening, we were unsettlingly
stoic. I remember going to a restaurant once and Ana, when she was
maybe eight or nine, asked the waitress, "What beverages do you
have?" The waitress cooed over someone so small asking something
that seemed so big. What third grader says "beverages"? I mean, I

get it. When my nieces, who are still too young to go to school, use any kind of social niceties, I lose my damn mind. A toddler asking "may I?" A baby making a tiny noise to indicate "please," widening the corners of their mouth like a smile when told to ask nicely. It's both so familiar and so foreign. It makes me want to cry and chant, "one of us, one of us."

Growing up, I remember feeling like the only thing worse than being called disruptive, disobedient, or rude was to be called any of those things in public. Our family could be disgusting and depraved around one another, in the privacy of our own home. We could fart at a concerning volume and burp on command. We could reminisce about how, when Frankie was three or four, he had a "booger wall"— the wall next to his bed where he stuck his boogers. We could see who in our family is flexible enough to bite their toenails—three of the six of us and not the three you'd expect. But the second we stepped out into the world, we had better act polite.

This was, in great part, because our family stuck out in most settings. We were usually the only family who wasn't entirely white, almost certainly the only family who was part Asian. There are also a lot of us. Most of my friends were one of two or three kids; four children, though not atypical of Catholic families in the late '90s, was an anomaly among our community. Our family of six would occupy most of a church pew. We often required an extra chair or two at restaurants. We just took up a lot of space, something that I think was uncomfortable for every member of our family of six, each of us someone who would shrink to the size of a Polly Pocket if it meant we'd make room for someone else.

Our instincts were to blend in, to follow the lead of someone with more gall and whatever gene made you taller than average. None of us really tried to be noticed because being noticed implied you were doing something differently than everyone else. Our existence was different enough; we didn't need to be seen as any more different than we already were.

This is the part of the story where I tell you my older brother, Zoey, has Down syndrome. Then comes the part where you say, "Oh, okay" in a way that doesn't seem too surprised or too positive, like you're overcompensating for it being a thing some people react to negatively. I know it's trite to say that Zoey is many things before and while being someone with a disability. He's a writer, an author, a musician, a movie aficionado, a brother, a son, an Elvis stan, and more knowledgeable on Stephen King, *NSYNC, and the entire cast of *Full House* (reboot included) than I am on anything. But I'd rather risk being trite and mention these things than brush past them and deny you the privilege of knowing a small part of who he is.

I try not to talk too much about and for Zoey when he's not in the room. Mostly because, when I do, I tend to cry out of a mix of love, protectiveness, guilt, and fear.* Also, because there are far too many people talking for Zoey as it is.

There are few things I fully hate—the smell of a grocery store seafood counter, playing video games that require me to move *and* look around *and* shoot. However, there is nothing so loathsome as the way popular media often uses disabled people, specifically people with disabilities that impact social behavior and cognitive function. I hate that "disabled" is treated as a monolith and always seems to mean the same thing: *okay, let's all be very careful now.* People with disabilities are condensed into a singular stereotype and

---

* I mention that specifically for the other people whose siblings have a disability. I think you get it, right? The complexity of trying to talk about someone you love without one million addendums, the simultaneous desire to scream at everyone and to shut up forever because it's not even about you? Everyone else, disregard and get out of this footnote.

used as props for other people's character development. They are examples of worse circumstances. They are trotted out as inspiration porn, put on display while they "overcome" their disability by doing something extremely regular. They are lauded only to say something about the people doing the lauding—How brave! How kind! How generous and noble! If one more person implies that Zoey, because he has Down syndrome, is a literal gift from God, I will self-immolate. How dare you deify our brother when me, Frankie, and Ana are right here, also looking heaven-sent and blessing you with our presence?

I suppose it's better than the alternative. My parents have heard people say things that no one should have to hear about anyone, let alone their child. Things that would hurt too much to write down or linger on for too long. The world is primed to disregard Zoey, to assume he can't or won't or doesn't or will never be able to. And rather than turn that assumption into cause for willing accommodation, for generosity, for grace, it's used to excuse everyone else's behavior.

The way my family thinks about manners is entirely tied to how we worry the world will think about Zoey. My mom once told me about an elementary school teacher who was pleasantly surprised that Zoey asked for a tissue after he sneezed. When Zoey says "please" or "thank you" or waits his turn or sits patiently or performs any kind of social nicety, it is too often, even still, met with surprise. (Mind you, he's in his early thirties.) Unlike when Frankie, Ana, or I do any of these things, Zoey is bucking expectations instead of meeting them.

And, while I understand that the world looks at Zoey and me very differently, I know the kinds of things perfectly nice people can say when they see someone doing something they find off-putting, uncomfortable, or different. I still assume that any unexpected attention I get is because I am doing something other people think is wrong. Because, again, I know the way that people can react when they see something they find surprising in a bad way. Thus, my instinct is to follow the rules, to mind my manners, to blend in and fall back and only speak up if absolutely necessary lest I call more attention to myself.

Not to make my brother's disability all about me—I say, after writing a thousand words about Zoey*—but the way I see goodness is inextricable from how the world sees him. I am hyperaware of the way an acquaintance interacts with Zoey, either being hesitant or overly familiar. I notice when the waiter addresses him as "buddy," the way someone a decade younger will ask him a question and look to my mom for an answer. (Again, Zoey is currently thirty-three.) I have seen the facade of performative niceness fall after that person turns away, the self-congratulatory smile when someone is— can you believe it—actually listening when Zoey talks. People know they should be nice to other people, especially when those people are disabled. They know not to say the r-word and, if they do, will apologize to me like I am the able-bodied gatekeeper of who can say what. I cannot help but be skeptical of other people's kindness, generosity, or goodness because what if they're putting on a performance on my behalf? What if they're just being considerate because they know they should be, because other people are around to

---

* Once, in college, I wrote a fictional short story about a brother and sister that was essentially a conduit for Zoey and me. The story was . . . fine and mostly exemplified my inability to write about anything that isn't directly tied to myself. During in-person critiques—something that should be a felony—a classmate said they didn't really "get" the story; they didn't understand why they should care about the characters, the plot, the intention, if it wasn't about a real person. Anyway, that's what I think about anytime I see a show with an able-bodied person playing a disabled character.

acknowledge their nobility? What if they give themselves a mental high five after doing a good job listening, after effectively pretending to care what I have to say? Because I ultimately can't help but make my brother's disability about me—at least in my own head—I am too often worried that people are showing me niceness because they feel bad, because they don't want to be mean despite their reflex to do so, because it will make them feel like a good person even if they aren't.

Of everyone in our family, I would argue that Zoey has the healthiest self-image. He is confident and excited to show off anything he's written, made, and done. He dances like everyone is watching and chanting, "Go Zoey! Go Zoey!" He has always loved and appreciated himself at a level that has taken me years of therapy and medication to even get close to. He knows that he's different from me and Frankie and Ana and not just because he's the only one of us who has memorized the entirety of *Jesus Christ Superstar*. I think that's something that surprises a lot of people, that Zoey knows he has Down syndrome. He understands he is a "person with a disability" and is aware that means he has limited access to much of the world. The *Jesus Christ Superstar* thing is not surprising at all; the man is deeply familiar with Andrew Lloyd Webber's entire body of work. I'd be more concerned if he suddenly couldn't perform Judas Iscariot's screamed solo on command.

For much of my life, I thought having manners, being considerate of others, and being well-behaved were one and the same, and all three were shorthand for being "good." Even though I was skeptical of others' kindness when it came to how they treated Zoey, dubious of their intentions when it seemed their goodness was performed, I, too, was putting on a one-woman show of performative goodness. Come one, come all, and see the young lady with zero self-examination! Ooh, ahh. Watch her mental gymnastics as she balances Looking

Good with Being Good. See her bend over backward for anyone in charge. For her next trick, she'll try to maintain the facade of being a Good Student, despite not doing the homework, by pulling an excuse out of her ass.

I believed Good Kids were polite and courteous. They held doors and shook hands. They didn't talk out of turn; they deferred to the adult in the room. And if they were asked to voice their opinion, they obliged but, in this and, well, every context, "opinion" meant "a regurgitation of whatever the present authority figure said." Because if you give your own opinion, it might be in disagreement with said authority figure. And it's rude to disagree, to argue—the two are the same, right? When people told my parents that we were "so good," this was often shorthand for "they're well-behaved and follow the rules."

Something I turn to over and over again is how manners directly overlap with ideas of obedience: both are about rule following, putting on certain airs, doing what some faceless authority figure has deemed correct. Even when they are about maintaining social niceties, they are still upholding some long-standing status quo; they are still following rules set in place by faceless authority figures. Do what Miss Manners said because she knows best. Do what Parents say because they are Parents. Do what President Daddy says because he is big, strong President Daddy.

Between injecting *Love Island* straight into my veins and googling "does my dog love me back," I managed to read a study on obedience. (Please clap.) In 2016, Matthew MacWilliams, a doctoral candidate at the University of Massachusetts–Amherst, conducted a survey about people's views on raising children. It asked either/ or questions about traits they'd want to foster in their kids: independence or respect for their elders; curiosity or good manners; self-reliance or obedience; being considerate or being well-behaved.

Those who favored the latter—respect, manners, obedience, being well-behaved—showed an inclination toward what psychologists deem "authoritarianism." Consequently, people who picked the latter option were also more likely, even among Republicans, to vote for Donald Trump in 2016.

Are the categories oversimplified and occasionally unrelated? Sure. There's certainly overlap between "being considerate" and "being well-behaved." Curiosity and having good manners don't need to be mutually exclusive. Still, the correlation seems telling. At least to me, an idiot who did some cursory googling.

The final traits mentioned are the ones that stuck with me the most: being considerate versus being well-behaved. Again, the two are linked if not combined into one, amorphous blob of niceness in my head. Can you be considerate while behaving badly? How can you behave well without being considerate? Why act polite if not under the guise of compassion? If anything, it makes me wonder who is expected to have manners and who they are expected to display those manners for?

Occasionally, my desire to question my own intention leads to me swinging too far in the opposite direction. I overcorrect, seeking catharsis by acting nasty as hell. I suppose it's only human. Who among us hasn't felt the impulse to rip off their clothes and stomp on a table amid an overly formal ceremony? How do any of us manage to suppress the desire to banshee-scream anytime someone tries to talk to us about NFTs? There is a physical, emotional, and spiritual release in behaving badly on purpose, and the same is true when we see someone who is supposed to be buttoned up doing something primal and stupid. The only thing I want to remember about the Trump administration is that Rudy Giuliani allegedly farted during a court hearing because . . . I mean, just read the words in that sentence. A grown man with a law degree ripped a beefer in an American institution dedicated to rules and regulations. Nothing could be funnier or more satisfying.

Though I am far too chickenshit to employ it regularly or even at all, there is something particularly delicious about pointed impoliteness. I have a mental shrine to the scene in *She's the Man* where Amanda Bynes is chompy-chomping a chicken wing after being told to "chew like you have a secret." I laugh compulsively when I think about Kim Kardashian swinging her purse at Khloe saying, "Don't be fucking RUDE." Imagine thumping someone in the head with a full bag while telling them to mind their manners.

Maybe it's more satisfying and cathartic to me, someone who has been primed to follow the rules, to mind my manners, to keep the book balanced atop my head. In preparation for my imagined debutante ball, I was not balancing the book with the goal of good posture; I was doing it solely to keep the book from falling. If I shrugged or wobbled or stuck my ass out stupid, who cares, because the end goal was merely to keep the book balanced. There was no deeper meaning, no bigger lesson. I did the thing I was told to do by the people who tell you to do things. The methods didn't matter, just the outcome. It's indicative of how I've thought of politeness, my greater ideas of obedience: my goal was rarely goodness; it was to be told I was doing a good job.

One of my favorite things about Zoey is that he burps and farts with reckless abandon. He'll belch midconversation while he's talking through a story he's writing. I'm sure he farted in front of Riley the first time they met. He's not doing it to be rude or as a kind of protest against social norms, though I'd like to pretend it's the latter. And no matter where the offense occurs—at home, at someone else's house, at a restaurant, during mass—Zoey will always, always excuse himself immediately after. Like both the act and the excuse are a reflex, a natural bodily function he can't keep in.

I think people would be surprised to know I've seen Zoey faking nice, though maybe not to the extent that I've feigned kindness. I've seen him smile through discomfort, sit quietly through a conversation he's not interested in. I've seen him eager to share an idea, a thought, a story, and wait until he's called on, if he's called on at all. He's learned to hold tight to his desire to be seen and heard and understood until he is told it's his turn. So, when I see someone slightly proud of themselves for listening to Zoey, for looking at Zoey, for seeing Zoey, it makes me want to shake loose any sense of my own decorum and ask whether they see Zoey has been playing along this entire time too.

It's a strange little dance we're all doing for each other, performing this balance of impulse and patience, participation and politeness. Zoey knows the moves better than anyone. But while he seems to be doing it for everyone around him, I feel like the rest of us are doing it for ourselves. Zoey does not need to be reminded he is good, kind, compassionate, but he knows he'll need to constantly show you that he is all those things. If you get to know Zoey, he knows you will like him, and he knows he'll probably like you, too. Oddly enough, I think that's where people so often misstep—they are not worried whether Zoey likes them because it is assumed. Zoey is trying to do the polite little dance with the person he's talking to, attempting to move through the conversation together, and too often the other person seems to be dancing for everyone else except Zoey.

Despite my own skepticism, I think I'd rather people fake kindness, act nice, say "please" and "thank you" than the alternative. I'd rather kindness be a reflex than have the instinct to say nothing at all. I'm not sure whether it's immediately harmful to pretend to be nice, to pretend to care. I'm not sure these kinds of performed niceties are inherently bad.

But when I am alone, and I think about the way I've moved or stayed still, shrank or spoken up throughout the day, the week, my entire life, too often I do not know who I've been doing this little performance for. I'm not sure why I put the book on my head. Too often I wonder something I'm sure Zoey has never had to question in himself: Have I been good or am I just acting nice?

WAYS I WILL DIE BECAUSE I DON'T WANT TO BE RUDE AND ASK FOR HELP

There is no certainty about what happens upon death. Is there life after this life? Is this all there is? How far is heaven and is it actually accessible by stairway? Fortunately, mortality is something I am fine with. I don't panic about it or feel the imminence of death when I realize it's 3:00 a.m. and I've somehow spent multiple hours watching teens explain how they keep their face looking dewy. Rather than ruminate on the unknown, I will speculate on something with a little more certainty: all the ways I will most certainly perish because I don't want to be a bother.

DEATH BY CHOKING

On an ordinary trip to a café, I order coffee and a bagel. I try to take a sip of the coffee knowing full well it's too hot. I burn my tongue and think, *Maybe the cream cheese will cool it down?* I think about licking the cream cheese but remember I'm in public. So I spread it on the bagel and quickly take a bite. The bite I take is far too big. I realize, oopsies, I'm choking. Rather than ask for help, I go into one of the single-stall bathrooms, lock the door, and await my inevitable death by suffocation and/or humiliation. When they find my body, I'll have tidied the restroom up a bit.

DEATH BY FRIGHT

I walk past a mirror and think I see a spider on my back. After sending myself into a full panic, I have an aneurysm. My ghost leaves my body, I look down at myself, and realize, *Oh, it was just the mole I've had on my shoulder my entire life.*

DEATH BY FALLING INTO A COFFIN AND BEING TOO EMBARRASSED TO YELL, "SOMEONE'S IN HERE!"

I love that, when we die, many of us will have our bodies put into gorgeous boxes. I love that the boxes go into the ground where no one gets to see them but at least they're expensive! One day, while window-shopping, I admire these gorgeous boxes, and accidentally trip and fall into one. As I never fully perfected the "occupied!" yell from the bathroom, no one hears my calm requests for help. Fortunately, dying while already in a coffin is a very polite way to go.

DEATH DURING CHILDBIRTH

The childbirth itself will not kill me. It's the embarrassment of shitting myself while pushing a baby out that ultimately leads to my death. Unfortunately, after I die, my body excretes poop, as is common upon dying. I die a second, even more humiliating death.

DEATH BY CURIOSITY

After spending the entire semester not taking part in class discussion, I finally raise my hand to ask a question. My teacher calls on me, happy he won't have to give me a zero in class participation.

Before I can answer, my cheeks become so flushed I combust, leaving a tiny pile of ashes behind with a small note that says, "Sorry!"

DEATH BY A THOUSAND CUTS

In the mood for a change, I go to get my hair cut. The stylist asks what I'm thinking and I say, "Just a trim. Or chop it all off. Or do whatever you want!" She says, "Really?" And I say, "Yep!" She gives me a gorgeous haircut and I feel so, so grateful. When I go to pay, I realize I don't have cash for a tip. The only solution is for me to spend the rest of my life repaying my debt by sweeping up the salon. One day, I slip on a big pile of hair and die.

DEATH BY THINKING TOO MUCH ABOUT DEATH

I fall into a rabbit hole, looking up all the ways bodies are displayed after death: a wake, a *Weekend at Bernie's* bender, as part of the "Bodies" exhibit where you're just muscles in the shape of someone playing basketball forever. I can't stop scrolling and clicking on Wiki page after Wiki page. I somehow die from the blue-light exposure. When my ancestors come to shepherd off my soul, they ask why I didn't just pay the extra twenty bucks for the blue-light-blocking protection on my glasses.

DEATH BY CHOCOLATE

I find an old piece of chocolate on the ground in the kitchen. I have an entire jar of new, unwrapped chocolate readily accessible in my pantry. But I decide to eat this floor chocolate anyway, just to see. It tastes fine. Kind of good even? I have no side effects and live a long life. On my deathbed, I wonder if I would have lived even a tiny bit longer had I not eaten that old chocolate one time years back. That brief moment of all-consuming panic drains the remaining bit of my life force and I die.

DEATH BY ATTENTION

After years of quietly wishing that everyone in the whole world would look at me for just one moment, they finally do. It is magical. We all feel an immediate connection and are transcended to a new plane of existence. We can each hear what everyone else is thinking, feel what everyone is feeling. We stop worrying whether we are trying too hard or not enough, faking nice or feigning confidence. It's glorious, euphoric. It feels like heav—oh, have I been dead this whole time?

Acknowledgments

Writing a book is hard, wonderful, embarrassing, and only possible with the help of many, many people who don't look at you crazy when you're like, "What if I . . . wrote a book?" If you enjoyed this book, it is in no small part due to the time, talent, patience, support, encouragement, group texts, kindness, and gorgeous brains of these people: Monica Odom, Sydney Rogers, Sun Paik, the entire Harper-One team, Hilary Swanson, Aidan Mahony, Rosanna Stevens, Elissa Bassist, Nneka McGuire, Irving Ruan, Camden Hanzlick-Burton, Margaret Hanzlick-Burton, my family, my parents, Zoey, Frankie, Ana, and Riley. If you didn't enjoy this book, you can blame my dog Ava, I guess.

I would also like to acknowledge a few more things this book would not have been possible without: the "Jazz Vibes" playlist on Spotify, Lexapro, sparkling water, the people who work at every coffee shop within a five-mile radius of my house, Justin's almond butter squeeze packets, Remi Wolf's "Monte Carlo," Wellbutrin, *PEN15*, TikTok, these chocolate-covered graham crackers I can't stop eating, sheet masks, weed gummies, and my bed.

Thank you! I love you each in a normal way!

About Mia Mercado

Mia Mercado is a humor writer whose work has appeared in places like *The New Yorker*, *McSweeney's*, *New York Times*, *New York* magazine's *The Cut*, and this book you are looking at right now. She lives with her husband, Riley, and dog, Ava, in Kansas City. If you want to see more of her work, you can follow her on Twitter @miamarket or Instagram @mia.market, but no worries if not!